1984

Meeting Educational N
of Young Adults

Gordon G. Darkenwald, Alan B. Knox, *Editors*

NEW DIRECTIONS FOR CONTINUING EDUCATION
GORDON G. DARKENWALD, ALAN B. KNOX, *Editors-in-Chief*

Number 21, March 1984

Paperback sourcebooks in
The Jossey-Bass Higher Education Series

Jossey-Bass Inc., Publishers
San Francisco • Washington • London

Gordon G. Darkenwald, Alan B. Knox (Eds.).
Meeting Educational Needs of Young Adults.
New Directions for Continuing Education, no. 21.
San Francisco: Jossey-Bass, 1984.

New Directions for Continuing Education Series
Gordon G. Darkenwald, Alan B. Knox, *Editors-in-Chief*

New Directions for Continuing Education (publication number
USPS 493-930) quarterly by Jossey-Bass Inc., Publishers.
Second-class postage rates paid at San Francisco, California,
and at additional mailing offices.

Correspondence:
Subscriptions, single-issue orders, change of address notices, undelivered
copies, and other correspondence should be sent to Subscriptions,
Jossey-Bass Inc., Publishers, 433 California Street, San Francisco
California 94104.

Editorial correspondence should be sent to the managing
Editor-in-Chief, Gordon Darkenwald, Graduate School
of Education, Rutgers University, 10 Seminary Place,
New Brunswick, New Jersey 08903.

Library of Congress Catalogue Card Number LC 83-82723
International Standard Serial Number ISSN 0195-2242
International Standard Book Number ISBN 87589-991-9

Cover art by Willi Baum
Manufactured in the United States of America

Ordering Information

The paperback sourcebooks listed below are published quarterly and can be ordered either by subscription or single-copy.

Subscriptions cost $35.00 per year for institutions, agencies, and libraries. Individuals can subscribe at the special rate of $25.00 per year *if payment is by personal check.* (Note that the full rate of $35.00 applies if payment is by institutional check, even if the subscription is designated for an individual.) Standing orders are accepted. Subscriptions normally begin with the first of the four sourcebooks in the current publication year of the series. When ordering, please indicate if you prefer your subscription to begin with the first issue of the *coming* year.

Single copies are available at $8.95 when payment accompanies order, and *all single-copy orders under $25.00 must include payment.* (California, New Jersey, New York, and Washington, D.C., residents please include appropriate sales tax.) For billed orders, cost per copy is $8.95 plus postage and handling. (Prices subject to change without notice.)

Bulk orders (ten or more copies) of any individual sourcebook are available at the following discounted prices: 10–49 copies, $8.05 each; 50–100 copies, $7.15 each; over 100 copies, *inquire.* Sales tax and postage and handling charges apply as for single copy orders.

To ensure correct and prompt delivery, all orders must give either the *name of an individual* or an *official purchase order number.* Please submit your order as follows:

Subscriptions: specify series and year subscription is to begin.
Single Copies: specify sourcebook code (such as, CE8) and first two words of title.

Mail orders for United States and Possessions, Latin America, Canada, Japan, Australia, and New Zealand to:
  Jossey-Bass Inc., Publishers
  433 California Street
  San Francisco, California 94104

Mail orders for all other parts of the world to:
  Jossey-Bass Limited
  28 Banner Street
  London EC1Y 8QE

New Directions for Continuing Education Series
Gordon G. Darkenwald, Alan B. Knox, *Editors-in-Chief*

Contents

Editors' Notes

Adults under age thirty-five comprise the majority of participants in organized continuing education. Despite this fact, the continuing education of young adults has received little attention in the professional literature. In contrast, there is an abundance of scholarly and professional writing on the distinctive characteristics and learning needs of the middle-aged and elderly. The present sourcebook is designed, in part, to help fill this gap. Thus, it complements the earlier New Directions volumes on *Programming for Adults Facing Mid-Life Change* (Knox, 1979) and *Programs for Older Adults* (Okun, 1982).

Like the earlier sourcebooks, this volume is based on the assumptions that adults at various stages of the life span differ in terms of salient developmental issues and tasks and that these differences should have a significant influence on the design of responsive educational programs. The general purpose of this volume, therefore, is to highlight the distinctive developmental attributes and tasks of the young-adult years and illustrate how continuing educators can use this information to develop or enhance responsive programs for young adults.

Although most of the contributions to this sourcebook deal with both theory and practice and the linkages between the two, the initial chapters emphasize theory and research findings in order to provide a general conceptual framework for interpreting the material that follows. Thus, the first chapter (by Merriam) provides an overview of the scholarly literature on young-adult development, and Darkenwald's chapter discusses research findings related to educational participation by young adults.

The remaining chapters, although they may draw heavily from research (as in Chapter 3 by Knox and Chapter 4 by Smith), deal primarily with the practical issues related to responsive programming for young adults. Each chapter is characterized by a distinctive focus, typically the needs and programming challenges posed by a particular subpopulation (for example, school dropouts, young parents, or young managers). In addition, each chapter addresses programs for young adults in a different organizational context, such as within the corporation, hospital, job-training program, or community college, and for different educational purposes. Despite this diversity in clientele, setting, and educational purpose, a number of recurring themes and issues emerge from a reading of this volume; these are identified and discussed in the concluding chapter.

We hope that this sourcebook will be of value to the field in two ways: first, by providing practical assistance to continuing educators who serve or

1

wish to serve young-adult learners and, second, by sparking a greater commitment among continuing educators to address the particular needs of this important segment of the adult population.

Gordon G. Darkenwald
Alan B. Knox
Editors

References

Knox, A. B. (Ed.). *New Directions for Continuing Education: Programming for Adults Facing Mid-Life Change,* no. 2. San Francisco: Jossey-Bass, 1979.
Okun, M. A. (Ed.). *New Directions for Continuing Education: Programs for Older Adults,* no. 14. San Francisco: Jossey-Bass, 1982.

Gordon G. Darkenwald is professor of adult and continuing education and codirector of the Center for Adult Development, Rutgers University. He has authored or coauthored numerous books and monographs, including Last Gamble on Education *(Adult Education Association, 1975) and* Adult Education: Foundations of Practice *(Harper & Row, 1982).*

Alan B. Knox is professor of continuing education at the University of Wisconsin–Madison. He is president-elect of the American Association for Adult and Continuing Education. His long-term interest in responsive programs for hard-to-reach adults is reflected in publications such as Adult Development and Learning *(Jossey-Bass, 1977) and* Programming for Adults Facing Mid-Life Change *(New Directions for Continuing Education, no. 2, Jossey-Bass, 1979).*

The issues and tasks that distinguish young adulthood from other periods of the life span have significant implications for continuing education.

Developmental Issues and Tasks of Young Adulthood

Sharan B. Merriam

A sourcebook called *Meeting Educational Needs of Young Adults* must be based on the assumption that young adulthood can be distinguished from other life stages. Indeed, research into adulthood within the last few decades supports the notion that young adulthood is qualitatively different from adolescence, which precedes it, and from middle age, which follows. Young adulthood is characterized by its own unique constellation of psychological issues and socio-cultural tasks.

The major psychological issues of young adulthood are those of independence, identity, and intimacy. These concerns manifest themselves in the broad arenas of occupation, family, and community. In each of these arenas, there are specific tasks, such as getting a job or becoming a parent, that are commonly encountered in young adulthood. Now, an individual issue, such as intimacy, or an individual task, such as getting married, can be (and often is) a concern of middle-aged and older adults. However, it is the *clustering* of these individual issues and tasks during young adulthood that sets this stage of adulthood apart from other stages.

Just when is young adulthood? Most writers say it begins somewhere in the late teens and ends by the early thirties. Several feel that it can be divided into two shorter periods. Bocknek (1980) writes about an introductory period

G. G. Darkenwald, A. B. Knox (Eds.). *Meeting Educational Needs of Young Adults.* New Directions for Continuing Education, no. 21. San Francisco: Jossey-Bass, March 1984.

(the ages eighteen to twenty-three) and the entry years (the ages of twenty-four to thirty-four). Chickering and Havighurst (1981) divide young adulthood into late adolescence and youth stages (age sixteen to twenty-three) and early adulthood (twenty-three to thirty-five). Other researchers (Levinson and others, 1978; Gould, 1972; Sheehy, 1976) pose even finer distinctions that include a transition from adolescence, the early twenties, the mid twenties (called "provisional adulthood" by Sheehy), becoming adult (Gould), and an age-thirty transition (Levinson and others). Many of these distinctions break down, however, when the variables of social class and sex are considered. Most working-class youth, for example, enter into a vocation and start a family sooner than middle- or upper-class youth.

The purpose of this chapter is to offer the reader an overview of the configurations of issues and tasks that distinguish young adulthood from other periods of the life span. Explored first are the psychological issues of independence, identity, and intimacy. Second, their relationship to the sociocultural tasks associated with occupation, family, and community will be discussed. Throughout the chapter, a conscious effort has been made to note how the interaction of psychological issues and sociocultural tasks is dependent, in part, on sex and social class.

Psychological Issues

The transition from adolescence into young adulthood is marked by diminishing preoccupations with self, peer status, and sexual development (Bocknek, 1980). Attention turns to finding one's place in the larger world, a task that requires the young adult to grapple with the issues of independence, identity, and intimacy.

Independence. Basic to the successful navigation of young adulthood is the achievement of psychological independence—that is, young adults must separate themselves from the protective security of their family of origin. As a child, a person is locked into the family unit in the same way a planet orbits the sun. Leaving adolescence requires a breaking out of this orbit or a "desatellization" in Ausubel and Kirk's (1977) terms. Desatellization from the family can be brought about by the "gradual replacement of parents by age-mates as socializating agents" (p. 131), by earning status in some adult role, or by assuming an "exploratory orientation" that carries with it the risk of developing values in conflict with one's family (p. 135).

Studies of adulthood have found the achievement of independence a major task for the young adult. Gould (1972), in a study of 500 middle-class subjects aged sixteen to sixty, identified two parts to the task: Leaving parents and breaking out is the first step; the second—leaving parents and staying out—occurs in the early to mid twenties. Sheehy (1976) in her interviews with young couples found "pulling up roots" to be the first task for young adults, followed by a period of "provisional adulthood." Sheehy also identified two conflicting needs among young adults—the need to be attached to others (to have the security that such attachment brings) and the need to explore, to become separate and independent. Females, she observed, felt a greater need to merge whereas males were conditioned to seek and explore. Finally, a study of men (Levinson and others, 1978) found "leaving the family" and "getting into the world" to be the major tasks of young men aged eighteen to thirty.

For most young adults, demonstrating some measure of independence involves a physical move out of the everyday presence of family. Some of them move into marriage or cohabitation; others join the armed services, take a job in another city, or attend college. Even students who are financially dependent on family are still learning to accept responsibility for their own lives and are developing values and mores independent of their parents' (Chickering and Associates, 1981).

Physically moving out does not, of course, automatically lead to psychological independence, nor does staying at home mean remaining forever dependent. More and more young people are finding living at home an economic necessity, and some move in and out as circumstances dictate. However much physically removing oneself from the family of origin contributes to achieving independence, it is not as important a factor as the young adult's psychological movement away from the family and toward a definition of the self as a separate identity.

Identity. A person's identity is what makes him or her a unique individual unlike anyone else. Adolescents experiment with many identities, often patterning themselves after adults they admire, and this trying on of identities alternates with submerging oneself into the peer group, hoping not to be singled out. Young adults on the other hand, begin to delineate a clearer sense of self, one that is more stable and less influenced by momentary attractions.

While nearly everyone knows intuitively what identity is, defining it so that its development can be studied has not been so easy. "Identity" has been variously wrapped up with notions of maturity, ego and moral development, and self-concept. Freud's famous definition of maturity as the capacity to love and to work, for instance, depends upon achieving a sense of identity versus remaining stuck in the role confusion of adolescence. One of Rogers' (1979, p. 47) criteria for maturity is having established a sense of identity—young adults "are aware of self, not in a self-conscious way but in a manner that allows them to act with self-respect. That is, the freedom to act is reinforced by the self-understanding, skills, and inclinations needed to act intelligently."

For some researchers, ego and moral development are critical components in one's evolving identity. Weathersby (1981, p. 52), in a review of the work on ego development, describes ego as "that aspect of the personality that 'keeps things together' by striving for coherence and assigning meaning to experience. The term *ego development* thus refers to a sequence, cutting across chronological time, of interrelated patterns of cognitive, interpersonal, and ethical development that form unified, successive, and hierarchical world views."

Jane Loevinger (1976), a distinguished expert on ego development, has identified eight milestones beginning with the "presocial" stage of infancy and ending with an "integrated" ego state. Although she does not correlate these stages to chronological age, her fourth stage of the "conformist" is typical of most adolescents and her fifth stage of "conscientious" ego development is congruent with young-adult identity formation. Unlike the conformist, who thinks and acts in cliches and absolutes, the person in the conscientious stage has become increasingly conscious of self, of multiple possibilities and choices, and has long-term goals and ideas.

Similar to Loevinger's conscientious stage of ego development is Perry's (1981) relativism stage of cognitive and ethical development. Perry defines cognitive and ethical development as "the evolving ways of seeing the world, knowledge and education, values, and oneself" (p. 78). In the relativism stage, the young adult tolerates diversity of opinion, values, and judgments and views knowledge as qualitative, dependent on context (p. 80). Similar findings have emerged from Kohlberg's (1976) studies of moral development; overall, his studies suggest a movement from self-centered moral reasoning, typical of childhood and adolescence, to reasoning based on a greater sensitivity to other people's perspectives and to the social context in general.

While identity cannot be defined solely in terms of ego, ethical, or moral development, research in these areas clearly suggests that the sense of identity in young adulthood involves moving away from a self-centeredness toward seeing how one fits into a broader context where there are many options for coping with the world. In summarizing the important change that occurs in identity formation between adolescence and young adulthood, Bocknek (1980) writes:

> Following from the intrapsychic disruptions of the adolescent identity crisis, a global reorganization seems to take place that is the first phase of identity formation. This is succeeded by a period of differentiation. These changes, from identity disruption through redefinition and reorganization and culminating in a self-construct that permits effective performance, describe a process that is probably necessary for human development in any cultural context. These developments in self-construct are critical. They condition the transition from child to adult [p. 183].

Intimacy. According to Erik Erikson (1950), the single most important task of young adulthood is to achieve an intimate relationship with another. Inability to do so results in isolation and loneliness. Identity, in Erikson's view, implies a structural integrity in which one is aware of the boundaries of the ego; the capacity for intimacy then, is based on "a sense of security about one's boundaries, such that 'fusion' with another person does not risk the loss of one's own identity" (Bocknek, 1980, p. 82). One cannot become close to another without sharing himself or herself, and "until the young person has developed at least a rudimentary identity, no whole self exists to be disclosed and to fully encounter another" (Douvan, 1981, p. 192).

For Erikson, the issue of identity is confronted in adolescence before dealing with intimacy in young adulthood, although vestiges of the identity formation process are present throughout the life span. In reality, the two tasks are probably not as sequential as his theory suggests. Young people who are in the process of separating themselves from their family, seeking emotional as well as physical independence, are also defining themselves as separate from all others. These drives of independence and identity run counter to attempts to merge with another, where total independence must be subsumed in the interests of the relationship. Schaie and Geiwitz (1982, p. 152), in addressing this problem, observe that "to a very large extent, maturity in young adulthood is a function of an individual's ability to balance the two opposing needs for independence and intimacy."

Intimacy can include a variety of physical and emotional experiences ranging from physical combat, to close friendship, to sexual intercourse. Douvan (1981) distinguishes between intimate relationships and role relationships and in so doing offers insight into how intimacy fosters growth in young adulthood. Role relationships, such as those between coworkers or among family members, are based on "shared expectations for behavior attached to positions in a social structure; they are affectively neutral, partial, and normative" (p. 191). Intimate relationships, however, do not depend on prescribed norms or expectations. "Value is attached to the partner and to the relationship itself rather than to some task or goal for which the relationship is instrumental." As a result, the individual "is freed to experiment with less known aspects of the self. . . . The intimate relationship is thus conducive to personality growth in a way that family relationships and other relationships heavily confined with normative expectations cannot be" (p. 191).

Although the issue of intimacy is one that recurs throughout adulthood, several of life's major decisions are based on the establishment of intimacy in young adulthood. Most young adults select a marriage partner, and some begin families of their own. Decisions affecting other areas of life, such as where and when to go to college, job selection, geographic location, and everyday living arrangements are heavily influenced by the presence (or absence) of an intimate relationship.

Sociocultural Tasks

The psychological development that a young adult goes through manifests itself in social behavior appropriate to the culture; that is, for any particular time in a particular culture, there are expectations that people will behave in certain ways. These expectations, or social norms, gradually change over time. Young adults in contemporary North America are expected to become financially self-sufficient through work, to set up a family unit of their own, and to make some commitment to the larger community.

Occupation. Choosing an occupation or preparing for a career is a nearly universal developmental task of young adulthood. Many factors, including family, peers, personal values, social class, and sex, influence a young person's choice of occupation. Most adults follow a relatively predictable pattern of work experience. In adolescence, one becomes aware of the options available and the preparation needed for various occupations. Young adulthood is traditionally a time of extended training or settling into a particular job or career. In the first years on the job, one explores the possibilities within the chosen setting or finds that the work is unsuitable and makes a change.

Levinson and others' study (1978) describes the components of occupational development for young men. The early tasks of career include selecting an occupation, forming a dream, and finding a mentor. The dream is an individual's expectation of what he will become, or would like to become, and is predominantly defined in terms of occupation.

For women, the progression of tasks in the arena of work is not so well defined. In the past, women's lives were structured in terms of childbearing and the stages in the family life cycle. In recent years, women have become increasingly career oriented and have increased their participation in the labor force dramatically (Chickering and Associates, 1981). For today's young-adult women, the question is not one of choosing between work and family but of how to combine marriage, motherhood, and work.

For most women, motherhood and sometimes marriage will mean periodic breaks in career. Bernard (1981) has delineated several "contingency" schedules typical of women juggling the concerns of family and work. The traditional sequence is one of school, marriage, family, and then work. For college-bound women, the sequence might consist of school, college, marriage, family, further training, and work, or some modification thereof. Of all possible variations, Bernard notes that "any schedule that interposes childbearing between professional training and career initiation would seem to be counterproductive" (p. 265). This schedule results in women attempting to enter the job market ill prepared and in competition with others who have a head start.

Attitudes toward work influence the choice of occupation of both young men and women. In a study of changing attitudes of young people from sixteen to twenty-five years of age Yankelovich (1974) found that attitudes toward work reflected a growing need for self-fulfillment. Young people want work to be meaningful and fulfilling and not just a means of supporting one's life outside work. "Three out of four of both college and noncollege young people call for more emphasis on self-expression and self-fulfillment as personal values" (p. 29). Among the highest-ranked job-related values held by blue-collar youth were seeing results of one's work, using one's mind, participating in decisions, and, most important of all, having work that is interesting. Yankelovich and others see problems, especially for noncollege youth, in finding work situations that match expectations:

That the majority of noncollege youth face the prospect of growing difficulties with their jobs must be regarded as a matter of serious concern to the society. These young people, after all, represent the great bulk of the new labor force. The problem they face is compounded by the multiplier effect of higher expectations with lower opportunities: Their New Values inevitably clash with the built-in rigidities and limited responses of the traditional work place [p. 37].

As with the psychological issues described earlier, preparing for an occupation is no longer an exclusive task of young adulthood. Due to changing technology and a changing economy, the average adult will experience three to five career changes in a lifetime (Hultsch and Deutsch, 1981). More flexible patterns of education, work, retraining, and leisure are also beginning to evolve. Growing awareness of these changes makes career planning for the young adult a more complex developmental task than ever before.

Family. The need to develop intimate relationships most often finds its expression through the establishment of the primary social unit — the family. This unit has a developmental cycle of its own, although the rhythm has changed somewhat over the last few generations. Today, people marry at slightly older ages, have fewer children, and divorce more often. Alternative family styles are emerging and the roles of husband and wife, father and mother are undergoing considerable change. Nevertheless, nearly all men and women in our culture marry at some point in their adult lives, usually in their twenties, and most have at least one child.

Young people marry for a variety of reasons. Biologically, marriage provides each partner with a regular sexual outlet, and young adulthood is the optimal time for producing children. Socially, there is a need to find someone with whom to share the work and expense of living independently of family. In a study of working-class couples, Rubin (1976) found that most fell into marriage largely because it was the thing to do at that stage in life. She quotes one man as saying, "I don't know exactly why I married her instead of somebody else. I guess everybody knows they're going to have to get married. I mean, everybody has to some time, don't they? What else is there to do but get married?" (p. 50).

Congruent with Rubin's findings are those of Sheehy's (1976), based on interviews with 115 middle-class subjects. Besides getting married because it was the thing to do, her interviewees expressed the need for a "safety net," or a need to fill some vacancy within themselves, or the need to get away from home. Not one of the men mentioned love as a factor.

The selection of a mate is dependent upon several variables or "filters," as one writer has theorized (Udry, 1974). The first filter is geographical propinquity—we select someone who lives near us. Next is the attractiveness filter, followed by screening mates on the basis of social background. Two people with similar social backgrounds further select on the basis of similar attitudes and values (the consensus filter) and then whether or not the relationship is complementary—that is, whether each "complements" the other's characteristics. Finally, people need to be ready for marriage. Readiness for a first marriage occurs in young adulthood.

Certainly not all young adults marry. Remaining single is much more of an option today than in the past. There are support groups, social institutions, and housing arrangements catering to the single person. Women who remain single are, as a group, better educated and of higher income and occupational status than their married peers (Rogers, 1979). Single young men, on the other hand, are less educated and of lower socioeconomic position than their married counterparts (Kennedy, 1978). For those singles who have not established any bond with other people, "singlehood represents the triumph of individual identity over interpersonal intimacy, and most of its disadvantages reflect the loss of what are gains in an intimate relationship. Loneliness is paramount" (Schaie and Geiwitz, 1982, p. 193). There are, however, many alternatives to marriage for sustained interpersonal relationships in young adulthood. Cohabitation, communal-family living, homosexual relationships, and participation in certain religious groups are a few such vehicles for achieving intimacy.

As with marriage, parenthood is a developmental task common to young adulthood that is undergoing change. Childless marriages, single parenthood, and delayed parenthood are becoming more acceptable options. Indeed, in a study of the saliency of Havighurst's developmental tasks, Merriam and Mullins (1981) found that young adults ranked having children as the least important task (out of eight) to be accomplished in young adulthood.

For those who do have children, childrearing affects their lives in different ways, based on social class and sex. Working-class couples, for example, have children at younger ages than middle-class couples. In one study (Russell, 1974), middle-class couples found parenting less rewarding than working-class couples. While fathering has received more attention of late, the major responsibility for childrearing in our society still resides with the mother. This fact results in women's career development or work life being interrupted by children while a man's is usually not (Bernard, 1981).

Community. The psychological issues and the social tasks of young adulthood necessitate the widening of a person's life to include the larger community—one's neighborhood, state, and nation. Becoming independent of one's family origin usually results in establishing residency in a community and thus depending upon the community for services and support. Working outside the home introduces adults to community and professional organizations related to one's job. Certainly marriage and especially parenthood lead to increased community involvement. "Familiar abstractions," Bocknek (1980, p. 108) writes, "now become concrete realities. Unemployment, birth control, legal rights—all of these become matters having implications for one's own action and well being."

This widening of one's awareness of the larger world is one of the characteristics of the maturing young adult. "World consciousness," as Bocknek (p. 108) calls it, "requires not so much an ability to name figures and current events as it does an awareness of the relationship between factors in the immediate world and one's own functioning." Robert White (1975), who has done extensive research on young adults, has also identified this "growth trend." He has labeled it an "expansion of caring"—that is, an expansion of oneself through serving others in the world community.

Growing civic concern further advances the process of independence and identity formation in young adulthood. Becoming politically aware and active may place one in conflict with parental values and generally accepted social norms. Periods of national crisis, such as the Vietnam War, exacerbate these tensions.

There is, of course, a range of participation in the larger community by young adults. Some may do no more than attend church, or pay taxes, or vote; others may join protest movements or run for office. Several writers have suggested that the range of involvement depends upon how orderly or stable one's work and family life are (Chickering and Havighurst, 1981; Wilensky, 1968). All maturing young adults, however, become aware of how impersonal outside forces, such as governments and social institutions, impinge upon their everyday lives (Bocknek, 1980). The task for each person is to accommodate these forces in such a way as to allow for continued personal growth.

Summary

Young adulthood is a distinct segment of the life span. It is characterized by a movement from the periphery to the core of adulthood. The movement requires young adults to "desatellize" themselves from their family of origin and become emotionally independent. This growing independence is accompanied by two other drives—one toward defining oneself as a separate, unique individual and one toward being able to establish close personal relationships with other people. These drives toward identity and intimacy are often in conflict with one another. It is out of this conflict that maturity evolves. The mature young adult arrives at a sense of himself or herself and at the same time learns to share this self with another.

The psychological issues of independence, identity, and intimacy are manifested in the arenas of work, family, and community. However psychologically independent a young adult might be, our culture requires that one also be a contributing member of society before adult status is conferred. Preparing for and starting an occupation, getting married and having children, and assuming some civic responsibility are earmarks of a socially mature person. Certainly not all young adults accomplish all of these tasks between their late teens and early thirties. There is also great variation in the timing of these tasks depending upon social class and sex. Nevertheless, this particular configuration of issues and tasks confronts all young adults, and it is this fact that makes young adulthood an identifiable stage of life, one for which continuing educators can plan meaningful programs.

References

Ausubel, D., and Kirk, D. *Ego Psychology and Mental Disorder: A Developmental Approach to Psychopathology.* New York: Grune & Stratton, 1977.

Bernard, J. "Women's Educational Needs." In A. W. Chickering and Associates (Eds.), *The Modern American College: Responding to the New Realities of Diverse Students and a Changing Society.* San Francisco: Jossey-Bass, 1981.

Bocknek, G. *The Young Adult.* Monterey, Calif.: Brooks/Cole, 1980.

Chickering, A. W., and Associates (Eds.). *The Modern American College: Responding to the New Realities of Diverse Students and a Changing Society.* San Francisco: Jossey-Bass, 1981.

Chickering, A. W., and Havighurst, R. J. "The Life Cycle." In A. W. Chickering and Associates (Eds.), *The Modern American College: Responding to the New Realities of Diverse Students and a Changing Society.* San Francisco: Jossey-Bass, 1981.

Erikson, E. *Childhood and Society.* New York: Norton, 1950.

Gould, R. "The Phases of Adult Life: A Study in Developmental Psychology." *American Journal of Psychiatry,* 1972, *129,* 521–531.

Hultsch, D. F., and Deutsch, F. *Adult Development and Aging.* New York: McGraw-Hill, 1981.

Kennedy, C. E. *Human Development: The Adult Years and Aging.* New York: Macmillan, 1978.

Kohlberg, L. "Moral Stages and Moralization: The Cognitive-Developmental Approach." In T. Lickona (Ed.), *Moral Development and Behavior: Theory, Research, and Social Issues.* New York: Holt, Rinehart and Winston, 1976.

Levinson, D., Darrow, C. N., Klein, E. B., Levinson, M. H., and Braxton, M. *The Seasons of a Man's Life.* New York: Knopf, 1978.

Loevinger, J. *Ego Development: Conceptions and Theories.* San Francisco: Jossey-Bass, 1976.

Merriam, S., and Mullins, L. "Havighurst's Adult Developmental Tasks: A Study of Their Importance Relative to Income, Age, and Sex." *Adult Education,* 1981, *31,* 123–141.

Perry, W. G., Jr. "Cognitive and Ethical Growth: The Making of Meaning." In A. W. Chickering and Associates (Eds.), *The Modern American College: Responding to the New Realities of Diverse Students and a Changing Society.* San Francisco: Jossey-Bass, 1981.

Rogers, D. *The Adult Years.* Englewood Cliffs, N.J.: Prentice-Hall, 1979.

Rubin, L. B. *The World of Pain: Life in the Working Class Family.* New York: Basic Books, 1976.

Russell, C. S. "Transitions to Parenthood: Problems and Gratification." *Journal of Marriage and the Family,* 1974, *36,* 294–302.

Schaie, W., and Geiwitz, J. *Adult Development and Aging.* Boston: Little Brown, 1982.

Sheehy, G. *Passages: Predictable Crises in Adult Life.* New York: Dutton, 1976.

Udry, J. R. *The Social Context of Marriage.* (3rd ed.) Philadelphia: Lippincott, 1974.

Weathersby, R. P. "Ego Development." In A. W. Chickering and Associates (Eds.), *The Modern American College: Responding to the New Realities of Diverse Students and a Changing Society.* San Francisco: Jossey-Bass, 1981.

White, R. W. *Lives in Progress*. (3rd ed.) New York: Holt, Rinehart and Winston, 1975.
Wilensky, H. L. "Orderly Careers and Social Participation: The Impact of Work History on Social Integration in the Middle Mass." In B. L. Neugarten (Ed.), *Middle Age and Aging*. Chicago: University of Chicago Press, 1968.
Yankelovich, D. *The New Morality: A Profile of American Youth in the 1970s*. New York: McGraw-Hill, 1974.

Sharan B. Merriam is associate professor of adult education at Northern Illinois University. Her latest book is Themes of Adulthood Through Literature, *Teacher's College Press, New York.*

Promoting participation by young adults requires understanding
their distinctive characteristics as a basis for program development.

Participation in Education by Young Adults

Gordon G. Darkenwald

Young adults (seventeen to thirty-four years of age) comprise not only the majority of participants in organized continuing education but their *rate* of participation also exceeds that of older age groups. In 1981, 54 percent of all participants were under the age of thirty-five, whereas this age cohort made up only 43 percent of the adult population (Kay, 1982). Among the reasons for the high rates of participation by young adults are their higher levels of educational attainment (the strongest predictor of participation in continuing education) and the immediacy, intensity, and wide scope of life-changing events that take place during young adulthood and that promote readiness to learn— such events as beginning a job, getting married, or becoming a parent.

Although young adults, especially those twenty-five to thirty-four who comprise 35 percent of all participants, are a "prime market" for continuing education, practitioners typically do not plan learning activities on the basis of the distinctive characteristics of this age group. If they did, not only would they attract even greater numbers of young adults but the education or training provided would also be more attuned to the needs of this group and thus more effective.

The purpose of this chapter, therefore, is to review the learning-related needs, interests, and preferences of young adults, their distinctive psychosocial and developmental characteristics, and the implications of these fac-

G. G. Darkenwald, A. B. Knox (Eds.). *Meeting Educational Needs of Young Adults.* New Directions for Continuing Education, no. 21. San Francisco: Jossey-Bass, March 1984.

tors for developing and marketing effective learning activities for this market segment.

Young adults cannot be treated as a single, amorphous category. Consequently, this chapter will emphasize differences based on relative age, sex, and socioeconomic status (SES). For example, a distinction is drawn between the "Stage 1" young adult (roughtly ages seventeen to twenty-four) and the "Stage 2" young adult (roughly ages twenty-five to thirty-four). Age parameters are always somewhat arbitrary, but there are three good reasons for using these particular categories in this chapter. First, the National Center for Education Statistics uses these categories in its analysis of national adult education participation data. Second, adults twenty-five to thirty-four years of age are generally responsible for their own lives and fully engaged in the roles that define adult status in our society; this is less true of persons aged seventeen to twenty-four. Finally, an abundance of research evidence (Bocknek, 1980; Chickering and Havighurst, 1981; Knox, 1977) indicates that the psychosocial characteristics and educational needs and interests of Stage 1 and Stage 2 young adults differ substantially.

Differences in socioeconomic status are mainly defined here by prior educational attainment and current occupational status for those aged twenty-five to thirty-four. For those seventeen to twenty-four, parental socioeconomic status needs to be taken into account, since many young people in this age range have not completed formal schooling or entered the job market.

Defining Young Adults' Reasons for Participation in Continuing Education

It is important to emphasize that few adults engage in an educational activity for only one reason or motive; instead, motives are typically mixed, comprised of constellations of related and sometimes unrelated discrete reasons (Darkenwald and Merriam, 1982). Because of this complexity, this section looks first at the more theoretical research on "learner types" and "motivational orientations"; we then use this information to interpret the specific reasons young adults give for participating in continuing education.

Houle's Typology. Using the in-depth interview method with a sample of twenty-two particularly active continuing learners, Houle (1961) identified three "types" of adult learner, which he described as follows:

> The first, or, as they will be called, the *goal-oriented*, are those who use education as a means of accomplishing fairly clear-cut objectives. The second, the *activity-oriented*, are those who take part because they find in the circumstances of learning a meaning which has no necessary connection, and often no connection at all, with the content or announced purposes of the activity. The third, the *learning-oriented*, seek knowledge for its own sake [pp. 15–16].

Although it is doubtful that there are only three or any exact number of pure learner types, House's formulation has at least intuitive validity. Probably his most provocative finding is that some adults (the activity-oriented) engage in continuing education for reasons, such as escape, stimulation, or social contact, that have little or nothing to do with acquiring knowledge or skills. Houle's small sample precluded generalizations about the relationship of his typology to age. However, subsequent research (Boshier, 1977; Cross, 1981) suggests that young adults are much more likely to be goal oriented than learning oriented. Activity/orientation, although not predominant, appears to be fairly widespread among Stage 2 women, particularly those who are socioeconomically advantaged.

Motivational Orientations. Houle's study led to a burgeoning of research concerned with testing his typology and identifying additional "motivational orientations." This work, epitomized by the research of Boshier (1971, 1977; Boshier and Collins, 1983), utilized questionnaires, large samples, and sophisticated statistical techniques. Boshier (1977), as well as others, have identified five general motivational orientation factors:

1. *Escape/Stimulation* — This factor reflects two related dimensions: a need to escape from routine, boring, or frustrating situations and a desire to find intellectual or social stimulation.

2. *Professional Advancement* — This factor more properly should be termed "occupational advancement" in that the items comprising it refer to work or jobs of any kind. It is strongly associated with improving one's occupational performance or status, reflecting a concern for acquiring useful knowledge, credentials, and job-related skills.

3. *Social Welfare* — High scorers on this factor enroll to gain knowledge or skills to help them achieve goals of societal or community betterment.

4. *External Expectations* — A degree of external compulsion or pressure is reflected in this factor. The individual is complying with the suggestions or requirements of someone else or some agency or organization.

5. *Cognitive Interest* — Those who score high on Cognitive Interest are identical to Houle's learning-oriented participants. They have the "inquiring minds" that value knowledge for its own sake, not for instrumental purposes.

Interestingly, motivational orientations seem to be only minimally related to age and not at all to sex. Boshier (1977) found a tendency for younger adults to enroll for External Expectations reasons and older adults for Cognitive Interest. The former finding might be explained by the greater control or influence that parents and employers exert over the lives of young adults.

Specific Job-Related Reasons. When asked specifically about their "main reason" for enrolling in a course or other organized learning activity, a majority of young adults respond in terms of getting a job or new job or improving or advancing in their current job. A recent national survey (Kay, 1982) reported that approximately 55 percent of Stage 1 and 70 percent of

Stage 2 young men enrolled for job-related reasons. The statistic for Stage 2 men (ages twenty-four to thirty-four) is perhaps startling but not difficult to understand. In contrast to younger men, these adults are less likely to require further education or training to *get* a job, are much more likely to be employed, and are often ready to move up to new responsibilities or better jobs. This interpretation is bolstered by the fact that nearly 80 percent of Stage 2 men further specified that their reason for participation was to improve or advance in their *current* job. Only 53 percent of Stage 1 men gave this specific job-related reason. These data support Chickering and Havighurst's (1981) contention that choosing and preparing for a career is the "most challenging developmental task" for Stage 1 men (p. 32), while starting in an occupation is the salient task for those in the Stage 2 age group.

The data for women show a similar but slightly less pronounced pattern of interest in job-related learning. Among younger (Stage 1) women, half attributed their participation in continuing education to job-related reasons (Kay, 1982). For Stage 2 women, the corresponding figure (unlike that for men) was only a slightly higher 56 percent. The obvious general interpretation for women's somewhat slighter interest in job-related education relates to their dominant developmental tasks. For many, particularly in the age range of twenty-five to thirty-four, not work but marriage, homemaking, and parenting are their most pressing life concerns.

For those women who do cite job-related reasons for participation, their reasons follow a pattern similar to that for men. Forty-five percent of Stage 1 women, compared with only 22 percent of their Stage 2 counterparts, report specific concern with getting a job or new job, not job advancement. As with men, interest in improving job skills or job advancement sharply increases with age: 52 percent of Stage 1 women specified participation for improving or advancing in their current jobs, compared with 71 percent of the more mature Stage 2 women.

Specific Nonvocational Reasons. Current national statistics (Kay, 1982) provide only a crude picture of nonvocational reasons for engaging in organized continuing education. For both men and women, nearly all report they are enrolled for "general education" or "personal and social" reasons. As one would expect, participation for general education reasons (such as to earn a diploma or degree) is considerably more prevalent for Stage 1 young men than for their older counterparts (54 percent versus 34 percent respectively). Although the age-related pattern for women is similar (35 percent for Stage 1 women versus 23 percent for Stage 2 women), it is clear that gaining a general education is a more important reason for participation for men than for women. The explanation, in part, is that more men than women are employed or seeking employment and need additional education to improve their job performance or to qualify for a job or for job advancement.

A striking, but not surprising, statistic is that 71 percent of the Stage 2 women who enrolled for nonwork-related goals specified "personal or social" reasons for participation. For Stage 2 men, the corresponding figure was 58 percent.

Finally, for both men and women at Stage 1, gaining a high school diploma, vocational certificate, or college degree was an important consideration for the large majority. For Stage 2 men and women, credits or credentials were considered important by only a third of the nonvocational participants.

The Relationship of Specific Reasons to Socioeconomic Status. Because national participation statistics have not been analyzed by direct measures of socioeconomic status (SES), it is necessary to use minority racial status as a proxy for SES. It should be stressed that race itself is irrelevant: High-SES blacks do not differ from high-SES whites in regard to their educational interests or level of participation (Darkenwald and Merriam, 1982). However, since black adults *in general* have less formal schooling, lower incomes, and lower status jobs than whites *in general*, it is justifiable to use race as a crude indicator of SES.

What we find is that a much larger proportion of black adults enroll for job-related reasons and especially to upgrade their "general education." The statistics cogently portray these differences, which are obviously due to socioeconomic inequality between blacks and whites. For example, of all the courses taken by white women in 1981, 35 percent were for "personal and social reasons." However, for black women, the corresponding figure was a mere 19 percent (Kay, 1982). Among black and other minority young adults aged seventeen to twenty-four, nearly all are enrolled in adult basic education, high school completion, or job-training programs. Survival needs, as Maslow (1954) pointed out long ago, always have first priority.

Conclusions Based on These Findings. In general, specific reasons for participating in a course or other learning activity reflect differences in the developmental tasks of Stage 1 and Stage 2 young adults and differences between young men and women. In terms of Houle's learning orientations, Cognitive Interest, or learning for its own sake, is largely the domain of the middle-aged and elderly. Young adults, both men and women, are overwhelmingly goal oriented; education is seen as instrumental to the achievement of specific competencies for performance in the adult roles related mainly to work and family life. This is particularly true of the youngest young adults. Stage 2 women and, to a lesser extent, men show more interest in personal-development objectives, many of which may be more expressive (such as painting or creative writing) than instrumental. Finally, the poorest, least-educated young adults participate, if at all, for survival reasons—mainly to obtain a high school equivalency (GED) diploma or the training required for getting a job.

Looking at the Effects on Participation of How and Where Learning Occurs

Although some research exists on the methods of learning that adults prefer and actually employ, few researchers have analyzed their data by age, sex, and SES. The same obtains for where adults prefer to learn and do actually learn, the "where" referring both to locations (such as at home or in a hotel) and to providing agencies (such as community colleges). Given the paucity of relevant research, this section will be brief and to the point.

Methods of Learning. The single most preferred and utilized method is the traditional lecture or class, preferred by 28 percent of adults and actually used by 35 percent (Carp, Peterson, and Roelfs, 1974). If self-directed education is excluded from the definition of participation, the percentage of adults learning in classrooms rises to 61 percent (Kay, 1978). Second in preference is on-the-job training, a method actually used by 14 percent of participants. Conferences, institutes, and workshops are preferred by 13 percent and utilized by 87 percent.

Although the traditional class still dominates adult education, it would be incorrect to conclude that adults prefer passive, traditional approaches to education. If one groups together all the methods that require active individual or group participation (such as on-the-job training, discussion groups, and workshops), it becomes clear that less formal methods are more often preferred and used by adults than formal ones. Differences in preferences do, however, exist. Darkenwald and Merriam (1982) note:

> Participation studies have consistently found that older adults, minorities, and adults with little formal schooling often dislike and avoid traditional classroom instruction. On the other hand, younger better-educated adults often prefer formal classroom instruction, no doubt in part because they are familiar and comfortable with traditional educational methods [p. 129].

For our purposes, what is most important about methods of learning and teaching is that they are appropriate to the aims and context of the learning activity. Some things are best learned by on-the-job training, and others in discussion groups or traditional classes. However, for young adults with limited formal schooling, especially school dropouts, it is wise to avoid the formal school-like methods associated with past failure and frustration. Not only do they "turn off" these young adults but it is also logical to assume that methods that failed in the past will probably fail in the future.

Locations for Learning. Adult education takes place everywhere — in community centers, YMCAs and YWCAs, churches, factories, museums, hotels, and, of course, in school and college classrooms. In general, young adults tend to study in more formal, conventional locations, particularly educational institutions. This is probably because the subjects that young adults typicaly study (that is, basic skills or vocational subjects) are part of what is normally provided by such institutions. Older adults, particularly those past sixty, prefer less conventional locations, such as community centers and libraries. One study (Carp, Peterson, and Roelfs, 1974) reported that learners under twenty-five were twice as likely as were older learners to utilize conventional locations.

As we might expect, men are slightly more likely than women to learn under the auspices of a business or industry (roughly 12 percent versus 8 percent). However, the proportion of men and women studying at two- and four-year colleges is roughly equivalent (Kay, 1982). One is tempted to conclude that location is an important factor in programming for older but not for young adults. There is one exception to this rule: Adults with little formal schooling, regardless of age, tend not to study or to want to study in formal educational settings, especially in colleges and universities (Darkenwald and Merriam, 1982).

Describing Barriers to Young Adult Participation

Like reasons for participation, barriers or deterrents are varied and complex. Few adults are dissuaded from participation because of a single barrier or problem. Instead, the barriers an adult confronts tend to take the form of idiosyncratic configurations, and their potency bears a direct relationship to the extent the individual is motivated to participate. Although little sophisticated research has been conducted to date on barriers or deterrents, most can be classified into four rough categories: situational, institutional, informational, and psychosocial.

Darkenwald and Merriam (1982, p. 137) describe situational barriers as factors that "relate to an individual's life context at a particular time — that is, the realities of one's social and physical environment." Cost and lack of time have been identified as by far the most serious situational barriers. Others include lack of childcare, transportation problems, and work schedule conflicts.

Institutional barriers are those "erected by learning institutions or agencies that exclude or discourage certain groups of learners because of such things as inconvenient schedules, full-time fees for part-time study, restrictive locations, and the like" (Cross, 1979, p. 106).

The category of informational barriers includes not only institutional failure to communicate information on learning opportunities but also, and more importantly, the failure of many adults, especially the least educated and poorest, to attend to, seek out, or utilize the information and information sources that are available.

Finally, psychosocial barriers are "individually held beliefs, values, attitudes, or perceptions that inhibit participation in organized learning activities" (Darkenwald and Merriam, 1982, p. 137). Adults who assert they "lack interest," are "too old to learn," are "tired of school," and the like are expressing psychosocial barriers to learning. These barriers are termed "psychosocial," rather than "psychological" or "attitudinal," to emphasize the role of social forces generally and of reference and membership groups specifically in forming and maintaining negative dispositions toward continuing education.

Age does not seem to have much bearing on the potency of institutional barriers, although they may pose slightly greater difficulties for older than younger adults. Informational barriers are serious obstacles to participation mainly for undereducated, low-SES adults, regardless of age. Situational barriers, in contrast, are related to both age and sex, and psychosocial barriers to SES.

As we have noted already, cost and lack of time are by far the most frequently cited barriers to participation. Not surprisingly, young adults under thirty-five and low-income adults perceive cost to be a much greater barrier than do older or more affluent adults. In addition, women are more likely than men to cite cost as a barrier. Lack of time, according to Cross (1981, p. 103), is mentioned "more often by people in their thirties and forties than by those younger or older, more often by the highly educated. . . and by those in high-income occupations." Of the other situational barriers, childcare stands out as a particular problem for young women but not, needless to say, for young men. Again, sex-defined developmental tasks and role expectations exert a strong influence on participation in continuing education.

Psychosocial barriers are related to age in that older, not younger, adults more often cite lack of interest, inability to learn, and lack of self-confidence as deterrents to participation. However, it is primarily among the least educated, the poor, and blue-collar workers that one finds the greatest psychological resistance to educational participation. Included in this group are disadvantaged or working-class young adults, school dropouts, and some noncollege-bound high school graduates. For such persons, as Darkenwald and Merriam note (1982, p. 139) "adult education may be seen as having little intrinsic value and little usefulness as a means of achieving personal goals. . . . The process of learning may be perceived as burdensome, unpleasant, or even frightening rather than as enjoyable or stimulating."

Recent Research on Deterrents. Before leaving the subject of barriers, we should mention the first attempt to identify global deterrent factors using the same mathematical procedures employed to identify motivational orientations (Scanlan and Darkenwald, 1984). Because the data for this study were obtained from questionnaires administered to allied health professionals, the results, described briefly here, are not generalizable to the total adult population. However, at least for occupationally related continuing education, they may be suggestive.

1. *Disengagement*—This factor comprises mainly psychosocial barriers, with in emphasis on passivity and indifference. Disengagement is more prevalent among women than men.

2. *Lack of Quality*—The items that comprise this factor indicate perceived deficiencies in current programs for health professionals (for example, "content not relevant," "wrong level for me," "unsatisfactory methods of instruction"). Younger professionals (aged twenty-one to twenty-six) rated this factor as less important than their older counterparts, who, it might be noted, had more experience as participants.

3. *Family Constraints*—The meaning of this factor is unambiguous—the

barriers consist of infringement on family time, childcare problems, and so on. As expected, Stage 2 respondents (aged twenty-seven to thirty-two) and women were most affected by family constraints.

4. *Cost*—Again, the meaning of the factor is clear. As might be predicted, younger (Stage 1) professionals and women were found to be most deterred by cost.

5. *Lack of Benefit*—This factor reflects a perception of no tangible or intangible "payoff" from participating in continuing education. It is not related to age or sex.

6. *Work Constraints*—Situational barriers such as work schedule conflicts, demands of the job, and "other commitments" characterize this factor. It is not associated with either age or sex.

It is noteworthy that the relationships between age and sex and the Family Constraints and Cost factors confirm the survey findings discussed previously. Also, Lack of Quality and, to some extent, Lack of Benefit, bear some resemblance to the category of institutional barriers. However, these factors are characterized not so much by inconvenient schedules or locations as by perceived deficiencies in the value of existing programs.

Conclusions. For young men, and especially women, cost is the principal self-reported deterrent to participation in continuing education. However, as Cross (1981) suggests, the cost barrier is probably exaggerated because few adults have any idea of actual costs or cost options and because there exists a discrepancy between the ability and the willingness to pay. Adults in general are willing to pay more for continuing education that enhances their career prospects than for learning opportunities geared to their personal development, intellectual stimulation, or proficiency in nonwork-related roles, such as parent, spouse, and citizen. Lack of time, on the other hand, is without doubt a serious constraint, especially for Stage 2 young men and women who are more fully engaged in work and family responsibilities.

Psychosocial barriers, such as negative attitudes and lack of confidence in one's learning ability, are more pronounced among older than younger adults and among the poorest and least educated irrespective of age. Recent high school dropouts, as well as some noncollege-bound graduates, comprise two of the hardest-to-reach segments of the adult population. Often indifferent or hostile toward education, frustrated and embittered by their experiences in school and also, perhaps, by chronic unemployment, and without self-confidence and encouragement from family and peers, they are not often eager to continue their education or likely to persist when they attempt to do so (Darkenwald and Larson, 1980).

Identifying the Implications for Programming

This section describes how practitioners can utilize information on the educational needs and developmental characteristics of young adults for program development and recruitment purposes. It is organized in terms of the two broad market segments: Stage 1 young adults, aged roughly seventeen to twenty-four, and Stage 2 young adults, aged twenty-five to about thirty-four. For discussions of the distinctive programming and recruitment implications for noncollege-bound young adults and for recent high school dropouts, see the chapters in this volume by Knox and Smith.

Stage 1 Young Adults. Although this age cohort is shrinking in size, the continuing education needs of these young adults are particularly urgent, and opportunities to respond to them are abundant. The most important fact for practitioners to remember is that most seventeen- to twenty-four-year-olds are undergoing the often painful transition from late adolescence or semi-adulthood to full adult status. Psychologically, they are consolidating their adult identity. As Bocknek (1980, pp. 171–172) puts it, "The focus of attention and energy now moves outward to a more refined world awareness," culminating eventually in the capacity for "long-term planning. . . [and] social awareness of obligation and responsibility."

The developmental tasks that relate to this period of transition include achieving emotional independence, preparing for marriage and family life, and choosing and preparing for a career (Chickering and Havighurst, 1981). Responsive programming needs to take into account the readiness to learn triggered by these transitions and tasks, as illustrated in Table 1.

As Table 1 suggests, most Stage 1 young adults are not especially in need of or interested in avocational programming, liberal education (such as Great Books discussion groups), or education for adult roles and responsibilities that are not imminent, such as becoming a homemaker or active in local civic affairs. For the most part, programming for this group should be oriented toward *preparation* for the responsibilities and opportunities of Stage 2 adulthood.

Table 1. Young-Adult Developmental Tasks and Educational Program Response

Tasks	Program Response	Outcomes Sought
1. Break psychological ties	1. Personal development; assertiveness training	1. Strengthened autonomy
2. Choose careers	2. Career workshops; values clarification	2. Appropriate career decisions
3. Enter work	3. Education/career preparation	3. Successful educational/ career entry
4. Manage home	4. Consumer education, homemaking skills	4. Informed consumer, healthy home life
5. Adjust to life on own	5. Workshops on living alone; successful singles workshops	5. Fulfilled single state; autonomy

Source: Adapted from McCoy (1977).

Provision should also be made in programs for this population for both career and personal-adjustment counseling. Counseling of the latter type, as Smith's chapter in this volume makes clear, is especially urgent for school dropouts. But other young adults, too, need guidance in dealing with difficult transitions, decisions, and problems that may interfere with learning or continued participation. One study (Lowenthal and others, 1975) describes men at this stage as often insecure, discontented, and lacking perseverance, and women as diffuse, dependent, and possessing a negative self-concept. As they enter young adulthood, women tend to develop a more complex lifestyle and "warmer" personal relations; they also tend to lack energy and to be jealous of activities, such as continuing education, that separate them from their husbands. Stage 2 men, in comparison, tend to become more expansive, buoyant, and risk taking. To some extent, then, programming should be segmented by sex role needs, interests, and developmental tasks.

Recruitment for this age group poses some difficulties in that many young adults cannot be reached easily by direct-mail promotion techniques. Most commercial or organization membership lists do not target school- and college-aged young people. Zip code or community mailings are also likely to be ineffective. Lists of recent dropouts or graduates can, however, usually be obtained from high schools. Advertising can be effective, especially through radio spots on stations that cater to this age group. Perhaps the cheapest and most promising recruitment strategy for many purposes is to work through the groups and organizations to which Stage 1 adults belong or have ties—the Cooperative Extension Service, Y's, churches, and so on.

Finally, practitioners should be aware of an enormous, virtually untapped market—the full-time student, one million of whom participated in adult education in 1981 (Kay, 1982). Even if recruitment efforts were confined to full-time college students, the potential market is about six million. The most obvious providers of noncredit learning activities for this group are the colleges' own continuing education units. However, other continuing education agencies that are reasonably accessible to a college population should weigh if and how they might serve the nondegree educational needs of this population. If approached in the right way, most colleges and universities will probably provide a mailing list of their full-time students. Other inexpensive and potentially cost-effective methods of promotion include advertisements in college newspapers or on college radio stations and the use of posters and flyers. Another strategy is to work with or through relevant college units, such as career counseling and placement, health services, and student affairs, to develop cooperative educational programs. Also, alumni organizations and their mailing lists should not be overlooked as a source for recruiting motivated young adults.

Stage 2 Young Adults. The Stage 2 cohort is not only large but also will continue to remain large for more than a dozen years as the last of the baby-boom generation matures. Containing 35 percent of all participants, it is the prime market segment for continuing education of all kinds in the 1980s and 1990s. An important fact for practitioners to keep in mind is that the learning needs and interests of this age cohort are extremely diverse, especially compared to Stage 1 adults and the elderly. Stage 2 adults are also extremely pragmatic. Learning for career advancement is the dominant motif for both men and women. In contrast to Stage 1 adults, there is also interest in this age group, especially among women, for continuing education oriented to avocational and personal-development objectives and to enhancing proficiency in adult life roles, such as spouse, parent, homemaker, and citizen.

For Stage 2 young adults, the transition to full adulthood is complete or nearly so, and emotional independence from parents and a sense of autonomous identity are solidified. The dependency, self-absorption, and self-doubt of the Stage 1 transition are replaced in Stage 2 by a sense of direction, self-confidence, and optimism. It is a period of "special sensitivity, readiness to learn, and multiple challenges" (Chickering and Havighurst, 1981, p. 34).

The cardinal principle of responsive programming, as with Stage 1 young adults, is to address the distinctive life changes and developmental tasks characteristic of this age cohort and of the specific segments within it defined by sex, occupation, life-style, and socioeconomic status. The informed practitioner can construct a model for responsive programming, such as that depicted in Table 1, for Stage 2 adults in general, Stage 2 managers, Stage 2 middle-class homemakers, and so forth. For the general Stage 2 population, for example, one might offer parent education workshops to help fathers and mothers adjust to or become more effective in their roles, or one might provide career-advancement training or job-redesign workshops to facilitate career development (McCoy, 1977).

Such examples are, of course, merely illustrative. Understanding the developmental characteristics of young adults, or of adults at any age, is valuable mainly for sensitizing practitioners to general issues and needs that are relevant to education. The research literature with all its information on these general issues is no substitute for professional creativity, the weighing of priorities and constraints, and the careful assessment of the educational needs and interests of clearly defined market segments.

Except for the socioeconomically disadvantaged and for blue-collar workers, traditional recruitment methods are effective with Stage 2 young adults. For the former, impersonal channels of communication, such as direct-mail promotion or advertising, simply do not work. To overcome their resistance or indifference, continuing educators need to work through or with the groups and organizations to which disadvantaged or working-class adults have ties—for example, unions, churches, community action agencies, and employers. General principles and examples of effective ways to employ such strategies are discussed in *Reaching Hard-to-Reach Adults* (Darkenwald and Larson, 1980).

Summary

Young adults, particularly those aged seventeen to twenty-four, differ in many respects from the middle-aged and elderly. They face distinctive developmental tasks that relate to preparing for, and later enhancing, their competencies in the work place and in the social roles characteristic of this stage of human development. Young adults are pragmatic learners — education is a means of preparing for and consolidating one's place in the world of work and family life. In contrast, liberal and avocational learning is principally the province of the middle-aged and elderly, when job and family demands are less multifaceted and urgent.

Despite many commonalities, young adults also differ in their educational needs and psychosocial characteristics due to such factors as relative age, occupation, sex, and social class. Not only are needs and interests related to these factors but so too are young adults' preferences for methods of learning and the barriers to their participation.

A better understanding of the educational needs, deterrents to participation, and developmental characteristics of young adults can be valuable to practitioners because it can provide the insight and sensitivity necessary to developing and promoting responsive programs. Such insight cannot, however, substitute for professional competence in designing and managing effective learning activities for a highly diverse young-adult clientele.

References

Bocknek, G. *The Young Adult.* Monterey, Calif.: Brooks/Cole, 1980.

Boshier, R. "Motivational Orientations of Adult Education Participants: A Factor Analytic Exploration of Houle's Typology." *Adult Education,* 1971, *21* (1), 3–26.

Boshier, R. "Motivational Orientations Revisited: Life-Space Motives and the Educational Participation Scale." *Adult Education,* 1977, *27* (2), 89–115.

Boshier, R., and Collins, J. "Houle's Typology After Twenty Years: A Large-Scale Empirical Test." Paper presented at the American Educational Research Association Conference, Montreal, April 11, 1983.

Carp, A., Peterson, R., and Roelfs, P. "Adult Learning Interests and Experiences." In K. P. Cross, J. R. Valley, and Associates (Eds.), *Planning Non-Traditional Programs: An Analysis of the Issues for Postsecondary Education.* San Francisco: Jossey-Bass, 1974.

Chickering, A. W., and Havighurst, R. J. "The Life Cycle." In A. W. Chickering and Associates (Eds.), *The Modern American College: Responding to the New Realities of Diverse Students and a Changing Society.* San Francisco: Jossey-Bass, 1981.

Cross, K. P. "Adult Learners: Characteristics, Needs, and Interests." In R. E. Peterson and Associates (Eds.), *Lifelong Learning in America: An Overview of Current Practices, Available Resources, and Future Prospects.* San Francisco: Jossey-Bass, 1979.

Cross, K. P. *Adults as Learners: Increasing Participation and Facilitating Learning.* San Francisco: Jossey-Bass, 1981.

Darkenwald, G., and Larson, G. (Eds.). *Reaching Hard-to-Reach Adults.* New Directions in Continuing Education, no. 8. San Francisco: Jossey-Bass, 1980.

28

Darkenwald, G., and Merriam, S. *Adult Education: Foundations of Practice*. New York: Harper & Row, 1982.

Houle, C. O. *The Inquiring Mind*. Madison: University of Wisconsin Press, 1961.

Kay, E. *Participation in Adult Education: 1975*. Washington, D.C.: National Center for Education Statistics, 1978.

Kay, E. *Participation in Adult Education: 1981*. Washington, D.C.: National Center for Education Statistics, 1982.

Knox, A. B. *Adult Development and Learning: A Handbook on Individual Growth and Competence in the Adult Years*. San Francisco: Jossey-Bass, 1977.

Lowenthal, M. F., Thurnher, M., Chiriboga, D., and Associates. *Four Stages of Life: A Comparative Study of Women and Men Facing Transitions*. San Francisco: Jossey-Bass, 1975.

McCoy, V. R. "Adult Life Cycle Change: How Does Growth Affect Our Educational Needs?" *Lifelong Learning*, 1977, *1* (2), 14–18, 31.

Maslow, A. H. *Motivation and Personality*. New York: Harper & Row, 1954.

Scanlan, C., and Darkenwald, G. "Identifying Deterrents to Participation in Continuing Education." *Adult Education Quarterly*, 1984, *34*, in press.

Gordon G. Darkenwald is professor of adult and continuing education and codirector of the Center for Adult Development, Rutgers University.

Findings from one of the few major studies on noncollege-bound
young adults suggest guidelines for more responsive continuing
education programs.

Serving the Noncollege Bound

Alan B. Knox

Out-of-school youth and young people who never attended college full time constitute the majority of young adults. Unfortunately, they are least well served by continuing education. Most providers mainly serve the young people who are most like college students. Annual participation rates increase with the level of formal education, from 5 percent for those who complete only a few years or less of school, to 25 percent of high school graduates to 50 percent of those with the equivalent of a master's degree or more (Johnstone and Rivera, 1965).

As a result, continuing education participation serves to widen the gap between the "haves" and the "have nots." One solution to this problem is for continuing education practitioners to gain a better understanding of non-college-bound young adults in order to create responsive programs for this group.

Late adolescence and early young adulthood are associated in the public mind with education (Bocknek, 1980). These are typically the college years, in which young people are full-time students in higher education institutions following high school graduation. The extent of formal education achieved is the characteristic most closely related to the extent of part-time and short-term continuing education that is sought throughout adulthood. The completion of high school and of each year of full-time postsecondary education is associated with higher participation rates in continuing education (Anderson and Darkenwald, 1979; Johnstone and Rivera, 1965).

G. G. Darkenwald, A. B. Knox (Eds.). *Meeting Educational Needs of Young Adults.* New Directions
for Continuing Education, no. 21. San Francisco: Jossey-Bass, March 1984.

Continuing education participation rates tend to be lower for adults during their late teens and early twenties (when the college bound are in school full time) than they are for the late twenties and early thirties, when participation associated with adaptation to new adult roles, along with higher participation rates by college graduates, combine to produce peak rates. The rates prior to age thirty would be even higher if it were not for the depressed participation of mothers who stay at home to care for their young children.

But what about the educative activity of the noncollege-bound young adults who drop out of high school or who graduate but do not complete more than a semester of full-time, post–high school education? Because going on to college for at least a year or two is mainly associated with family affluence, the majority of young people who do not are more representative of their age group than might be anticipated.

Social class, then, helps differentiate the extent of educative activity by college-bound versus noncollege-bound young adults. But what are the salient correlates of extent and type of educative activity among the noncollege bound? This was the focus of the major national study upon which this chapter is based (Knox, 1970). In addition to informal information seeking and to learning projects that used print and electronic media and conversations with other people, the study included all forms of part-time and short-term educational activity regardless of content, method, or provider (Johnstone and Rivera, 1965; London, Wenkert, and Hagstrom, 1963; Parker and Paisley, 1966). Examples included occupational education provided by an employer or the military, part-time courses provided by educational institutions, study discussion groups provided by religious institutions or community agencies, patient education provided by hospitals, and workshops provided by associations.

This chapter presents the explanations about participation in continuing education by noncollege-bound young adults that emerged from this study and from the few similar studies that have been conducted (Carson, 1965; Hendrickson and Foster, 1960; Horner and Knox, 1965; London, Wenkert, and Hagstrom, 1963; Super and Associates, 1967; Trent and Medsker, 1968; Waldron, 1968). Salient correlates with participation occurred in relation to past experience, current relationships, and personal outlook (Sewell and Associates, 1969). This chapter looks at each of these three categories of correlates, then looks at the patterns of relationships across categories, and concludes with a section on the implications for practitioners.

Past Experience

The noncollege-bound young adults varied greatly in their experience prior to adulthood, and various aspects of their past experience were associated with the extent of current continuing education activity. As previous research cited above indicated, most of the noncollege-bound young adults in

Knox's (1970) study had fathers with blue-collar jobs and no formal education beyond high school. By contrast, young adults from higher-status families acquire more education, both full time and part time. Thus, social class strongly differentiates the college bound from the noncollege bound. How does it relate to participation in continuing education activities? Among the noncollege bound, parental family status variables (such as levels of educational and occupational attainment) were not highly associated with the young adult's educational *participation* (although the father's level of occupational prestige was associated with the young adult's expressed *interest* in continuing education).

By contrast, adolescent home environment of the noncollege-bound young adults varied greatly and, as researchers anticipated, was one of the variables most highly associated with the extent of current continuing education activity. These home environments varied from abundant to impoverished regarding books, reading, and the use of library materials. The abundance of the adolescent home environment was positively associated not only with the extent of current educative activity but also directly or indirectly with most of the other variables associated with participation. The fathers' level of occupational prestige was associated with home environment, even though it was little associated with the young adult's current educative activity. There was also an association among the young adult's verbal ability, home environment, adjustment, and amount of time spent reading magazines.

Noncollege-bound young adults varied greatly in their general adolescent activity level in terms of recreation, jobs, and nonschool-sponsored education. A high general adolescent activity level and more engaged life-style were moderately associated with the extent of current educative activity, even though individual variables such as working or recreation were not. However, the extent of out-of-school educational activities during high school years (such as public library use and learning through youth group projects) was positively associated with the extent of current continuing education participation. As previous research had led us to expect, feelings about high school were not greatly associated with actual participation in continuing education but were associated with the extent of expressed interest in participation.

Current Relationships

The young adults varied greatly in their current role relationships, and the extent of their involvement in various roles was positively associated with the extent of educative activity. They tended to have lower-prestige occupations and to have somewhat lower levels of role performance and satisfaction than more highly educated adults. About half belonged to no organizations, compared with about one third of adults generally, and those who did belonged to fewer organizations and were less often in leadership positions.

The extent of current educative activity was associated with leisure styles that were active and that included reading, cultural activities, and community participation. The highest correlate of educative activity was the extent of organizational participation, which was in turn associated with adolescent home environment and current magazine reading. However, organizational participation was not highly associated with job-related educational activity, and level of occupational prestige was not associated with variation in educative activity but it was associated with interest.

The other people whom the young adults perceived as most significant or important to them were typically relatives or residents of the same neighborhood. Few "significant others" were associated with job or organizational settings. Significant others were typically older than the young adults but had about the same amount of education. Most were perceived by the young adult to feel that the young adult should obtain more education, and even more of them were perceived to feel that education was very important. In addition to a strong association with actual participation, the proportion of significant others who urged the young adult to obtain more education was the highest correlate with interest in continuing education (Booth and Knox, 1967).

Personal Outlook

The outlooks of noncollege-bound young adults were oriented toward the present and the future, and they included abilities, self-concept, and attitudes toward self and work. Their outlooks were in some respects more variable than for the general adult population. There was evidence of somewhat more need for affiliation and somewhat less personality integration than for adults generally, which probably reflected the adjustment problems of young adulthood. There also was slightly less happiness, security in groups, and activity out of groups. This conflict in self-concept and moderate self-satisfaction was especially characteristic of the most active continuing education participants. This was an indication of their recognition of discrepancies between current and desired proficiencies (Bocknek, 1980; Knox, 1980).

The intellectual abilities of the most able noncollege-bound young adults were well within the range of college students. Contrary to expectations, ability was only slightly related to educative activity and to general functioning. As anticipated, ability was less associated than socioeconomic status with educative activity. Vocabulary level was somewhat associated with educative activity, especially with participation in continuing education provided by educational institutions (in contrast with programs provided by employers).

Social and emotional adjustment is a global concept related to many variables associated with participation, but its direct relation was not to formal continuing education participation but to informal information seeking and especially to magazine reading. As anticipated, adjustment was associated with expansiveness and performance in the roles of worker, organization member, and user of leisure. Adjustment was also associated with an abundant adolescent home environment, the need for affiliation, thoughtfulness, planfulness (which was associated with verbal ability), and the selection of an autonomous favorite leisure activity. Contrary to expectations, planfulness was not associated directly with educative activity but was associated indirectly through adjustment, low adherence to authority, positive feelings toward school, perception of reading as a desired job characteristic, organizational participation, preference for autonomous leisure activities, and a reading orientation.

The association between continuing education participation generally and both reading orientation and organizational participation reflected for the noncollege-bound the familiar barriers to participation faced by most adults who seldom read and who belong to no voluntary associations. Most continuing education activities have implicit rules, as do other organized groups, and they depend on reading; thus, they tend to discourage people whose lifestyle does not include these activities. For the young adults who were only engaged in job-related continuing education, there was less of an association with a reading orientation and more of an association with optimism about promotion chances. However, other attitudes toward their current job were little related to the extent of educative activity. Optimism about promotion was also positively associated with both adjustment and work satisfaction.

Patterns of Relationships

Some of the basic conclusions from the study spanned the three categories of variables. Educative activity by noncollege-bound young adults was significantly associated with various personal and situational characteristics related to past experience, current relationships, and personal outlook toward the future. In other words, there was not one or a few variables that were highly associated with the extent of educative activity; it was the *number* of facilitating variables more than the types of variables that differentiated between participants and nonparticipants. There appears to be a threshold for continuing education participation, such that three or more major facilitating variables (with at least one personal and one interpersonal) will result in participation. This reflects a transactional basis of motivation to participate, in which both personal inclinations and situational factors are influential. It is important to remember that, although social class and intelligence may differentiate the college bound from the noncollege bound, these two variables were not major predictors of the extent of educative activity among the noncollege bound. A combination of other variables had stronger and more direct relationships with participation.

The transactional pattern of related variables is illustrated by the following two composite clusters of variables that were highly associated with the extent of educative activity by noncollege-bound young adults. These clusters can be called an "engaged life-style" and an "idea orientation."

Some of the young adults in the study seemed to have a more active, curious, *engaged life-style* than the others, and these young adults were more likely to be involved in continuing education. Associated characteristics included growing up in a more abundant home environment; having achieved high-status occupations; and currently tending to be more autonomous, planful, and thoughtful about ideas. Also associated was expansiveness, as character-ized by active coping and social adjustment and by assertion, achievement, and expansion of life space in a variety of domains (such as through organiza-tional participation).

The *idea orientation* was characterized by an emphasis on reading and thoughtfulness about issues of self and society. Reading of books and maga-zines was more central to the leisure style of participants than nonparticipants. This may help explain why twice as many significant others of the participants urged them to obtain more education than was the case for nonparticipants. Perhaps evidence of an idea orientation (such as reading and interest in issues) encourages significant others to urge young adults to obtain more education.

These two patterns emerged for almost all categories of noncollege-bound young adults, regardless of region, community size, and race. How-ever, there were several ways in which the young women in the study differed from their male counterparts. They were more reading oriented, had a some-what different leisure style, and experienced somewhat different career devel-opment (Mulvey, 1963; Trent and Medsker, 1968). Regarding reading orien-tation, they liked school better, described a more book-oriented adolescent home environment, spent more time reading magazines, and were more inter-ested in an ideal job that included reading. Regarding leisure style, they belonged to fewer organizations, their favorite leisure activity was more other directed, their leisure role performance ratings were lower, and fewer of their significant others urged them to obtain more education. Regarding career development, they held higher-status occupations (not necessarily higher pay-ing), but their worker role performance ratings were lower, and they were less optimistic about their chances for promotion.

For both male and female noncollege-bound young adults, there were small age-related differences that seemed to reflect developmental trends during late adolescence and early young adulthood, indicative of a maturing process (Knox, 1977). With age, the older young adults were progressing occupationally (as reflected in higher-status occupations, higher worker role performance ratings, and higher work satisfaction); became more reading oriented (as reflected in more time spent reading magazines, higher vocabu-lary test scores, and more interest in an ideal job that would entail reading); were more socially engaged (as reflected in belonging to more organizations and in higher ratings on leisure role performance and social adjustment); and were gaining greater mastery over their environment (as reflected in greater orientation toward planfulness and achievement).

Most of these relationships were consistent with findings from the small amount of previous research and the predictions of experts, especially regarding the importance of a reading orientation and of the encouragement of others. The low direct relationships between participation in educative activity and both social class and intelligence were not anticipated.

Implications for Practice

Based on the overview presented in the preceding sections are the following major implications for continuing education practitioners who want to develop responsive programs to attract and serve noncollege-bound young adults.

1. Relate Programs to Adult Roles to Encourage Participation. Educative activity was positively related to performance in the worker role and to organizational participation. Some young adults combined organizational and educational participation, while others appeared to rely on organizational coping strategies instead of more formal educative activity. The latter young adults used coaching and informal orientation to enhance their proficiency while avoiding the book orientation and structure of more formal continuing education. Thus, practitioners can include people who interact in work, church, organization, or informal group settings in the process of planning educative activities that are based on their shared organizational experience and commitment.

In addition to informal learning projects and group discussion, practitioners can emphasize educational methods that relate learning to life roles; such methods include case-study exercises, role playing, and action learning.

One way to encourage participation by current nonparticipants is to begin with change events (such as marriage or a job promotion) that can trigger participation by producing a heightened readiness to learn (Aslanian and Brickell, 1980). Another spur to participation are discrepancies between current and desired proficiencies as reflected in only moderate job satisfaction and perceived conflicts in adjustment and self-concept; in the study, these were associated with the extent of educative activity. Practitioners can help nonparticipants clarify discrepancies that nonparticipants believe they can deal with, using strategies that alternate between action tasks and relevant educational resources (Smith, 1982, 1983).

2. Capitalize on Developmental Trends of Young Adulthood. Adult growth and development is most likely when the setting encourages the changes a person wants to achieve (Knox, 1977). This transactional and developmental process was reflected in the study in the shift toward more engagement and an idea orientation during late adolescence and early young adulthood. Substantial motivation and development were reflected in increasing occupational development, mastery over the environment, role differentiation, social engagement, and reading orientation.

People are more subject to influence when they are changing (Bocknek, 1980). The many major role changes of young adulthood produce a heightened readiness to learn that practitioners can use to encourage such young adults to engage and persist in educative activity. Marrying, parenting, changing jobs, moving, or joining an organization entails inescapable uncertainty, adjustments, and questions (Knox, 1977). Practitioners can help young adults to include educative activity as part of the natural problem-solving process. For example, acceptance of new responsibilities in a job or organization that entail careful reading can encourage efforts to increase reading speed and comprehension, which might be viewed as unimportant under other circumstances. Parenting can stimulate interest in community and value questions and in child development. Job expectations can help a young adult focus on new skills to be mastered for continued employment and advancement.

3. *Accommodate the Distinctive Developmental Patterns of Young Women.* In addition to having somewhat different approaches to career development, leisure role, and reading, young women engaged in educative activities that were more separately clustered around work or leisure. Practitioners can provide programs focused on these separate interests and, in these programs, can rely more on books and reading. Continuing educators can also help young women make plans that fit their interests and circumstances, including making adjustments in program arrangements to accommodate student, work, and family roles.

4. *Appeal to the Multiple Influences That Can Be Strengthened.* Various personal and situational variables were associated directly or indirectly with participation in educative activity. Some of these potential influences are easier to reinforce and strengthen than others in order to encourage further educative activity by recent participants and similar young adults. For example, the highest correlate with continuing education participation generally was the extent of organizational participation, which in turn was influenced by the abundance of the adolescent home environment and by the extent of planfulness. While it is impossible to go back in time and enrich the adolescent home environment of current young adults, it is possible to encourage them to join an organization and to emphasize planfulness in both work and organizational activity as useful prerequisites to more formal educative activity.

Other characteristics highly associated with interest or participation have potential for marketing purposes. Examples include a reading orientation and encouragement by significant others. To increase the encouragement of significant others, a continuing education provider can cosponsor educational activities with an organization to which the young adults already belong; sometimes just adding one more "facilitator" (such as the leaders of the organization) will result in participation.

In addition, marketing efforts can focus on significant others and reference groups related to family, work, religious or secular organizations, or informal social groups. Marketing messages aimed at these significant others can encourage them to talk with noncollege-bound young adults to increase awareness of opportunities, stress the value of education, facilitate initial enrollment, urge persistence, and assist the young adults to use what they learn (Knox and Associates, 1980).

Nonparticipants may also be attracted to informal programs (that lack an emphasis on reading and the formal structure of a voluntary association), which may be more compatible with their current life-styles.

5. Each Provider Agency Should Serve the Types of Young Adults It Most Readily Attracts. Although there is substantial overlap, various providers attract adults with somewhat different characteristics. For example, verbal ability was associated with participation in continuing education provided by educational institutions but not with that provided by employers. Knowledge of the clientele of various agencies can indicate which provider is most likely to attract an underserved segment of young adults. Employers, labor unions, urban recreational centers, occupational training programs for the unemployed, the military service, community colleges and technical institutes, the Cooperative Extension Service, penal institutions, and religious institutions can each make a distinctive contribution. Cosponsorship by such providers may further increase involvement of nonparticipants.

6. Adapt Arrangements to the Client's Life-Style to Attract the Harder to Reach. The noncollege-bound young adults who recently participated in continuing education activities were quite similar to those who went on to college full time. You will probably need different approaches to attract and serve current nonparticipants (Darkenwald and Larson, 1980). Successful approaches will compensate for lower levels of aspiration (by clarifying discrepancies between current and desired proficiencies), of organizational participation and encouragement by significant others (by increasing reference-group support), of reading orientation (by avoiding reading as a prerequisite and developing it as a concomitant), and of occupational prestige (by recognizing limited ability to pay and providing subsidy as needed). Successful approaches are likely to entail practical learning-by-doing methods in concrete situations with direct applications.

7. Strengthen the Continuum of Preparatory and Continuing Education. Although it is impossible to go back and change the early life experiences of current young adults, it is possible for continuing education to be aimed at parents, teachers, and youth-group leaders who work with children and adolescents so that these young people enter young adulthood with a stronger orientation toward lifelong learning. For example, in-service education programs for teachers could emphasize learning how to learn and positive attitudes toward self-directed learning projects as well as content coverage. Parent education programs could emphasize the contribution of a reading-oriented home environment to the child's subsequent development. Teachers of youth groups could be helped to appreciate how influential informal learning projects are on later educational participation.

Public stereotypes sometimes center on social class or minority groups or on differences between rural and urban backgrounds. It is important to recognize how little such differences are associated with the extent of educative activity among noncollege-bound young adults. By contrast, continuing education practitioners *can* do something about the major correlates, such as reading and idea-oriented home environments, encouragement by significant others, organizational participation, and recognition of discrepancies between current and desired proficiencies (Knox, 1980).

Summary

This chapter does not present continuing education practitioners with a simple explanation of a few major influences on the extent of educative activity by noncollege-bound young adults. However, it does offer practical suggestions based on an understandable rationale.

The continuing education participants are differentiated from nonparticipants by a more engaged life-style and greater orientation toward reading and ideas. The various correlates of participation reflect a transactional, developmental process in which past experience, current relationships, and personal outlook interact. Evidence of developmental maturation includes increasing occupational development, an orientation toward reading, social engagement, and a mastery over the environment.

Major past-experience correlates of participation include the abundance of the adolescent home environment and the extent of adolescent out-of-school educative activity. Major current-relationship correlates include organizational participation and the extent of encouragement by significant others to obtain more education. Major personal-outlook correlates include a reading orientation, occupational dissatisfaction, and (for job-related continuing education) optimism regarding promotion.

Practitioners should feel optimistic that current influences (such as organizational participation, occupational opportunities, and encouragement by significant others) can override past influences (such as negative feelings about school or the low socioeconomic status of parents).

In short, the research indicates that responsive educational activities for noncollege-bound adults must relate directly to practical tasks associated with role performance and adjustments. The list of references suggests further reading for practitioners interested in strenthening educational programs for this large group of young adults.

References

Anderson, R. E., and Darkenwald, G. G. *Participation and Persistence in American Adult Education.* New York: College Board, 1979.

Aslanian, C. B., and Brickell, H. N. *Americans in Transition: Life Changes as Reasons for Learning.* New York: College Board, 1980.

Bocknek, G. *The Young Adult.* Monterey, Calif.: Brooks/Cole, 1980.

Booth, A., and Knox, A. B. "Participation in Adult Education Agencies and Personal Influences." *Sociology of Education,* 1967, *40* (3), 275–277.

Carson, R. P. *Factors Related to the Participation of Selected Young-Adult Males in Continuing Education.* Unpublished doctoral disseration, Florida State University, 1965.

Darkenwald, G. G., and Larson, G. A. (Eds.). *New Directions for Continuing Education: Reaching Hard-to-Reach Adults,* no. 8. San Francisco: Jossey-Bass, 1980.

Hendrickson, A. and Foster, E. *Educational Needs of Out-of-School Youth in Columbus, Ohio.* Columbus: Ohio State University, 1960.

Horner, J. T., and Knox, A. B. "Encouraging Noncollege-Bound Young Adults to Participate in Continuing Education." *Adult Leadership,* 1965, *14* (6), 186 ff.

Johnstone, J. W. C., and Rivera, R. *Volunteers for Learning.* Hawthorne, N.Y.: Aldine, 1965.

Knox, A. B. *Factors Related to Educative Activity by Noncollege-Bound Young Adults.* Final Report, United States Office of Education Project 6-1826. New York: Teachers College, Center for Adult Education, Columbia University, 1970.

Knox, A. B. *Adult Development and Learning: A Handbook on Individual Growth and Competence in the Adult Years.* San Francisco: Jossey-Bass, 1977.

Knox, A. B. "Proficiency Theory of Adult Learning." *Contemporary Educational Psychology,* 1980, *5,* 378-404.

Knox, A. B., and Associates. *Developing, Administering, and Evaluating Adult Education.* San Francisco: Jossey-Bass, 1980.

London, J., Wenkert, R., and Hagstrom, W. O. *Adult Education and Social Class.* Berkeley: Survey Research Center, University of California, 1963.

Mulvey, M. C. "Psychological and Sociological Factors in Prediction of Career Patterns of Women." *Genetic Psychology Monographs,* 1963, *68,* 309-386.

Parker, E. B., and Paisley, W. J. *Patterns of Adult Information Seeking.* Stanford, Calif.: Stanford University, 1966.

Sewell, W. H., and Associates. "The Educational and Early Occupational Attainment Process." *American Sociological Review,* 1969, *34,* 81-92.

Smith, R. M. *Learning How to Learn.* Chicago: Follett, 1982.

Smith, R. M. (Ed.). *New Directions for Continuing Education: Helping Adults Learn How to Learn,* no. 19. San Francisco: Jossey-Bass, 1983.

Super, D. E., and Associates. *Floundering and Trial After High School.* Final Report, Cooperative Research Project No. 1393. New York: Teachers College, Columbia University, 1967.

Trent, J. W., and Medsker, L. L. *Beyond High School.* San Francisco: Jossey-Bass, 1968.

Waldron, M. W. *A Study of Selected Background Factors and Their Relationship to Participation in Adult Educational Activities of Young Adults from Rural Areas.* Unpublished doctoral dissertation, University of Wisconsin, 1968.

Alan B. Knox is professor of continuing education at the University of Wisconsin-Madison. His research and writing related to noncollege-bound young adults and to participants in adult basic education reflect a conviction that the field should give greater attention to less-advantaged adults.

For young adults aged seventeen through twenty-one, the developmental challenges particular to their age cohort are intensified by high school dropout status and require the emphatic attention of continuing educators.

High School Equivalency Preparation for Recent Dropouts

Franceska B. Smith

Except on those occasions when nostalgia overwhelms our rememberance of things past, how many of us would truly wish to be late adolescents again? The late-adolescent to young-adult years between seventeen and twenty-one are difficult ones—a developmental limbo in which one is scolded for being childish but treated as not quite grown-up enough to assume full adult role responsibilities and privileges. Young people are viewed by their elders with a mixture of envy and disdain as they struggle to find their way into full-fledged adulthood. Moreover, the developmental stresses inevitable in the earliest stage of young adulthood are exacerbated if one faces uncertain employment because of low literacy, lack of job-related skills, or discrimination or if one has children of one's own to care for. And surely another exacerbating condition faced by millions of young adults today is the status of high school dropout.

Young dropouts have much to contend with, and they must endure social stereotyping to boot. Dropouts are at an ever-increasing disadvantage. In the first place, school completion rates have climbed from perhaps 10 percent at the turn of the century to approximately 80 percent in the 1960s, where they remain today. Education and training opportunities frequently require graduation from high school. So do many entry-level employment opportunities, particularly in large cities as their economies shift from manufacturing to white-collar service jobs. A high school diploma is now, as Larson (1982) sug-

G. G. Darkenwald, A. B. Knox (Eds.). *Meeting Educational Needs of Young Adults*. New Directions for Continuing Education, no. 21. San Francisco: Jossey-Bass, March 1984.

gests, a minimum credential for full participation in adult life. And, as both Darkenwald and Knox note in other chapters in this volume, the extent of formal education completed is associated with higher rates of participation in continuing education.

Even though continuing education is shunned by most young-adult dropouts, adult basic education (ABE) and high school completion (HSE) programs are experiencing an influx of young adults who lack a high school credential. Although, as discussed in the next section, precise data cannot be obtained, there is a discernible and accelerating trend toward an increasing proportion of very young adults, age seventeen to twenty-one, enrolling in these programs. This trend is discussed by Muraskin and Fischer (1975) and Lant (1977), among others. These authors note that many continuing educators view the trend warily, fearful of high schools "dumping" their intractable students into public supported programs for adults — programs that are already overcrowded and underfunded.

Continuing educators are not exempt from the public perception of the young adult dropout as a social problem. Like most stereotypes, this perception has a measure of truth. Program staff and state education department personnel who supervise continuing education may fear that by their behavior, even by their very presence in classrooms, very young adults will drive away older adult students and even staff who fear the crime and vandalism committed by unemployed, out-of-school youth. Apprehension may also be fueled by another public perception — that is, that high school standards and student achievement have declined over the years and that, therefore, recent dropouts will be more academically disadvantaged than older adult dropouts enrolled in the same high school completion programs.

This chapter reports a case study of young adults aged seventeen through twenty-one in a high school equivalency (HSE) program sponsored by a community college. Like any case study, this one has limited generalizability. However, it is presented in the hope that it may alert continuing educators to issues they might consider in programming for young dropouts in this age cohort who are not enrolled in postsecondary education. It may also suggest some ways that program practice can be improved.

Qualitative as well as quantitative data are reported in an effort to convey the flavor of how people in this age group interact with older students and staff, how they are perceived by others, and how they interpret their own experience. Quantitative data alone, no matter how precise, provide incomplete information. Surely our understanding of a 36 percent dropout rate in the case study, for example, is enhanced by a sense of how much more anxious and easily discouraged this cohort is than HSE students over age thirty. One twenty-year-old woman interviewed for the case study compared high school equivalency to the liquid protein diet (evidently a quick and unpleasant means to a desired goal!). After offering this analogy she added, "I'll do anything I have to, as long as it doesn't take too long. I've just got to get back on track!"

Getting "back on track" was a recurrent theme among the young people interviewed, and one of the purposes of this chapter is to explore some of the meanings they assign to it.

Setting: The Institution and the Program

Garden Community College (a pseudonym) is a public, urban institution located in a middle-income residential community. The students in Garden's high school equivalency program resemble those in the college's degree programs; they are of working-class background as well as lower-middle-income (blue-collar, sales and service, civil service) and approximately 30 percent minority. The similarity is not surprising in view of the fact that 50 percent of Garden's HSE graduates go on to college, and, of these, half attend Garden Community College. However, the average age of Garden's HSE student is slightly lower than that of degree program students who have an average age of twenty-five or so. The slow but steady decline in the average age of HSE students is attributable to a recent influx of younger, school-age dropouts, aged seventeen to twenty-one, who now constitute over half of Garden's HSE enrollment.

In this respect at least, Garden's high school equivalency program is typical of most. The young-adult influx in high school equivalency and adult basic education results from a combination of factors, including high school dropout rates that are especially high in large urban centers, job-market pressures, and changes in laws governing compulsory high school attendance. These factors are considered in *Giving Youth a Better Chance: Options for Education, Work, and Service* (Carnegie Council on Policy Studies in Higher Education, 1980).

Lant (1977) provides an interesting explanation of the peculiar alliance that supports (1) lowered age requirements both for high school exit and for eligibility for enrollment in high school equivalency programs and (2) General Educational Development (GED) ("equivalency") testing. This alliance encompasses deschooling advocates such as John Holt; the Kettering Commission, which described compulsory attendance laws as "the dead hand on the high schools"; and fiscal conservatives. The conservatives, according to Lant, "influenced by fast-rising school costs, have been impressed by a reported yearly saving in California of between $3 million and $3.5 million directly attributable to lowered eligibility for the proficiency examination [California's own equivalent of the GED]. They have hastened to support similar measures in their own states" (p. 54).

Young-adult influx is a trend, then, but it is exceedingly difficult to get a handle on it in order to generalize about individual states or the nation as a whole. Reliable data on high school equivalency enrollments and student age are simply unavailable. In contrast to adult basic education (a federal program), high school equivalency is sponsored and usually funded in full or in part by states (and by other providers, each with a different funding source and not under the jurisdiction of state education departments). The National Association for Public Continuing Adult Education (NAPCAE) survey (National Association for Public Continuing Adult Education, 1982) suggests a current HSE enrollment of about 700,000 in state-sponsored programs, but it provides no estimates of student age.

More complete data on the age of test candidates (people who take the GED tests) are provided by the GED Testing Service. This agency of the American Council on Education oversees the development of the six-and-one-half-hour examination for which high school equivalency registrants are preparing. The GED Testing Service administers the "equivalency" testing program cooperatively with designated officials in each state's department of education, which awards high school certificates on the basis of test results.

However, any inferences from GED Testing Service data on test candidates to high school equivalency students must by made very cautiously. The two populations overlap but are not the same. For example, only half of a 1980 sample of test candidates had previously enrolled in a high school equivalency class (Malizio and Whitney, 1981). On the other hand, GED Testing Service data can be suggestive; for example, they reveal a gradual decline in the average age of test takers from twenty-nine during the 1960s to twenty-five currently (General Educational Development Testing Service, 1982). These data also reveal that nearly 40 percent of test candidates nationally are seventeen to nineteen years old.

Except for the age of its students, in most other respects the program at Garden Community College is atypical of high school equivalency programs. Although, as Grede and Friedlander (1981) suggest, community colleges are making inroads as providers of noncollegiate adult education, the typical provider of high school equivalency is the public school district. Local districts offer HSE free or at low cost several evenings a week, usually using public school classrooms and employing part-time administrators and teachers, many of whom work in the day schools. State tax-levy monies and, very occasionally, local funds are used to supplement federal funds available through amendments to the 1966 Adult Education Act. Of course, there are exceptions (programs sponsored by two-year colleges, correctional institutions, the military, businesses, unions, civic groups, and so on), but the small public school program run on a shoestring is the prevailing pattern.

Garden's HSE program is unusual with respect to its size, cost efficiency, diagnostic-prescriptive emphasis, and differentiated instructional placement. Educational counseling is an essential part of Garden's program. (Few other programs are large enough to provide all the services, such as career counseling and college adapter classes, that help make Garden Community College's program so successful. The final section of this chapter, however, suggests some low-cost ways that Garden's success might be emulated.)

It is likely that the program's location on a college campus attracts an ambitious, upwardly mobile clientele eager for the expedited college admission that the program provides its successful students. This promotes self-selection of students likely to successful. A required reading level of at least an eighth-grade equivalent and a per-semester fee of between $40 and $50 are other factors affecting the makeup of the student population.

A Broad-Brush Portrait of Younger Students

In most essential respects, the subjects of this case study, seventeen- to twenty-one-year-olds at Garden Community College's high school equivalency program, did not fit the worst stereotypes of the disadvantaged dropout or fulfill the worst fears of wary program staff. They did not cause disruptions on campus or in classrooms. They did not scare off middle-aged students or staff, although, as will be described in the next two sections, in various and subtle ways the classroom behavior of the youngest students provoked teacher dissatisfaction. In physical appearance and dress, the seventeen- to twenty-one-year-olds were nearly indistinguishable from the slightly older, twenty-five to thirty-year-old adults. Because of this fact and in order to highlight developmental and psychosocial differences, the comparisons reported here contrast seventeen- to twenty-one-year-olds (a total of thirty-eight) with fellow students over thirty years of age (of which there were fifty-three). "Over thirty" is both a popular epithet and a convenient demarcation of mature adult status.

In marked contrast to the stereotype of the "dumb" dropout who left high school after repeated academic failure, the young adults admitted to Garden's high school equivalency program showed surprisingly solid skills in reading and math. Fully 30 percent of the case study sample of seventeen- to twenty-one-year-olds achieved grade equivalent scores of at least 11.0 on a placement test in reading taken during registration. Math placement scores were typically two years lower, but sufficient for the math portion of the GED battery. It should be noted that placement test scores in this range, rough indicators as they are, would enable many adults to pass the GED tests and obtain a state-sponsored diploma without any formal preparation whatsoever. Other academic advantages enjoyed by the youngest adults in the case study included recency of schooling and familiarity with multiple-choice tests.

Despite their comparative academic advantage over older students, however, the very young adults in Garden's HSE program did not fare as well as would have been expected. Of those with the highest reading placement test scores, 60 percent of those who persisted in the program obtained satisfactory scores on the GED. This compares with 70 percent of the "over-thirty" students with comparable placement test scores. (Across all levels of achievement, however, the middle-aged students' scores on tests taken early in the program may be slightly depressed. The "over-thirty" cohort's achievement may, therefore, reflect an increase in test-taking skills.) At the lowest level of reading placement test scores (grade equivalents of 8.0 to 9.5), only 14 percent of the seventeen- to twenty-one-year-olds persisted and made sufficient progress to pass the GED, compared with 30 percent of the older students at this level.

Of course, the appropriateness of grade equivalent scores in adult education is open to debate, but clearly the lower overall "success rate" of the younger students is cause for concern. Success rate (the percent of those enrolled who actually obtain a diploma) is considered here rather than pass rate for several reasons. First, pass rate (expressed as the proportion of those who pass versus the total number scheduled for the test) is dependent in part on the accuracy of predictor measures and counselor judgment in making test referrals. If only the very "best bets" are referred to take the test, the pass rate will be correspondingly higher. Second, success rate takes account of attrition. And since pass rates were relatively similar for younger and older students matched for reading ability, the lower success rate of the seventeen- to twenty-one-year-olds is attributable in large part to their higher attrition rate.

The problem of younger students' attrition was apparent throughout the duration of the ten-week program. For instance, to the distress and bewilderment of program staff, 13 percent of the youngest registrants never came back after the first night. A few of these were young people who would have been scheduled to take the GED immediately. Another 16 percent drifted away after a few weeks. The youngest students displayed a cumulative drop-out rate of approximately 36 percent (compared with 28 percent for "over-thirty" students).

In addition, the case study data suggest differential rates of perseverance. To any student who did not achieve the required standard scores the first time he or she took the GED tests or who failed to appear for the exam as scheduled, the program offered counseling, the opportunity to audit specific classes as needed, and expedited rescheduling for the exam. Only 30 pecent of the youngest students returned after their first failure, compared with 40 percent of those over age thirty. And of all those who took the test a second time, 70 percent of the older students passed, compared with 52 percent of the younger students.

Differences in success rates, dropout, and perseverance between younger and older students are further illuminated by some additional contrasts described in the next section. Some of these are reported in terms of perceptions because perceptions (attitudes and expectations) are especially important to understanding better a learner group that is frequently subject to stereotyping.

Further Contrasts Related to Student Age

Both survey and interview data provide a sense of the frank dissatisfaction of young adults with their high school experience. One third of the survey sample reported that they had dropped out of high school because of boredom. (Older adults, by contrast, omitted the item entirely or chose more socially desirable options such as "I needed to get a job" or "family problems.") Few respondents in either age group indicated low grades as their main reason for having dropped out. In interviews, seventeen- to twenty-one-year-olds mingled criticism of their high schools ("a complete zoo," "I was afraid to go to the restroom," "even when I tried, when I was doing everything really great, it all seemed, like, useless") with self-criticism ("I admit it, I had a bad attitude"). It seemed that they were very ambivalent about high school, often abhoring it but berating themselves for forfeiting opportunities offered by high school graduation. This was particularly true of young people who had endured a humiliating succession of dead-end jobs after dropping out. Moreover, ambivalence about high school seemed to transfer to high school equivalency— about which more will be said shortly.

As to their main reason for seeking a GED diploma, 58 percent of the youngest students (compared with 49 percent of the older students) indicated they wanted a diploma in order to seek admission to college. Almost equal percentages of younger and older students sought the diploma for personal satisfaction or work-related reasons. What these data do *not* reveal is the urgency felt by young adults in pursuit of a diploma. Time and again they spoke desperately of the diploma as a way of getting "back on track," as if dropping out of high school had been a derailment of an orderly progression toward vocational and social status as adults. Pressure from parents and significant others (relatives, friends, employers) was alluded to ("my mother says she's going to put me out"). However, in the main, the motivation to succeed was described as a response to the realities of the job market—by young women as well as young men. An associate (two-year) college degree was considered a necessary ingredient in vocational preparation, and this might account for the predominance of "college" over "work" as the main reason given for seeking a high school equivalency diploma.

As to how they had learned of Garden's high school equivalency program, student responses also differed by age. This divergence, summarized in Table 1, might be of particular interest to anyone wishing to assess the effectiveness of different recruiting strategies according to the age of the target population.

Data in this table demonstrate the importance of word of mouth in attracting HSE registrants of all ages. The value of the HSE graduation ceremony as a recruitment strategy—with full regalia of caps and gowns, a brass band, and speeches by local dignitaries—is also apparent. The data suggest that adults' organizational affiliations are not a significant source of information about HSE opportunities.

It also appears that local high schools are starting to refer students in informal ways; this item was of particular interest to program staff concerned with "dumping." What this survey did not query but should have was whether employers or coworkers were sources of information about Garden's HSE program. Finally, mention should be made of the fact that, although the entire

Table 1. Student Survey Responses as to How They
Learned of the HSE Program

	Percent of Respondents Selecting Each Option[a]	
	Students Aged 17–21	Students Over Age 30
Survey Option	(N = 38)	(N = 53)
Continuing education catalogue	33	49
Newspaper ad about HSE program	13	21
Relative	31	23
Friend/neighbor	36	40
School attended by respondent's children	0	4
Church or Temple	0	4
Civic or community group	0	9
College's HSE graduation ceremony	18	13
Guidance counselor at respondent's high school	18[b]	0

[a] Totals for each group exceed 100 percent because more than one option could be selected.
[b] Of younger students with the lowest reading scores, 28.6 percent selected this option.

survey was anonymous, respondents were asked to provide their zip codes. The zip code data facilitated a rudimentary kind of market analysis. It was possible, for example, to begin assessing the effectiveness of the catalogue as a promotional device or the predominance of high school "referrals" in a given residential area.

The survey revealed a consensus among students of all ages, and among program staff as well, that the classroom behavior of seventeen- to twenty-one-year-olds is distinctive, not to say deficient. This consensus was corroborated by interviews and observations. Among the characteristics ascribed to very young adults was, first of all, a tendency to cut HSE classes "when they're tired or have something better to do." The youngest respondents agreed with this assessment of themselves, as they did with assertions that younger, more often than older, students are inclined to "get bored with classwork occasionally and daydream or talk with friends" and also to drop out of the program altogether. Younger adults were also seen as less "willing to work hard" than older students (a view they themselves subscribed to) and not as good as older students at planning and managing their learning in the program.

My experience as participant-observer tends to confirm this consensus of perceptions. Analysis of attendance records revealed irregular attendance by younger students; observation confirmed occasional lapses in classroom decorum. Assessing someone else's "willing[ness] to work hard" involves often quite subjective inferences from behavior, but poor planning at the very least was evident in the tendency of many of the youngest students to forget their textbooks, notebooks, and sometimes even their pencils. Younger students were generally less likely to do homework when assignments were given.

Of course, there were always notable exceptions to any of the generalizations advanced here. For instance, some of the young women who were hardly out of their teens, particularly those aspiring to secretarial or nursing careers, copied down practically every word on the chalkboard and were punctilious about completing each assignment or exercise.

Younger students also participated in class discussions less frequently and with less enthusiasm than older students. They volunteered fewer answers in response to teachers' questions. They rarely addressed anyone, except the counselors, by name. The teachers' somewhat cantankerous interpretation of younger students' classroom behavior is presented, along with other participants' interpretations, in the next section.

A final note is in order concerning the survey items that probed perceptions, almost all of which displayed statistically significant differences in the way that younger and older students were viewed. One item pair elicited the perception that younger students are less able than older students to produce clear, correct expository prose. This was of interest (even though the GED tests do not include a writing sample) because of the discovery, in the course of the case study, that young adults as a group were indeed seriously deficient in writing ability, although most were articulate in conversation. Consequently, a writing skills unit was included in the program along with other newly-instituted units on job-seeking skills. These instructional units were provided to students awaiting their test scores. It was explicit program policy, carefully explained to all registrants, that they would be referred to the exam as soon as they were judged "test ready" by the counselors on the basis of placement and diagnostic/predictor test scores. The supplementary instructional units have proved reasonably effective in stemming attrition by those awaiting test results.

If seventeen- to twenty-one-year-olds are found wanting in almost every comparison with their older peers, how can the high aspirations of these young adults be reconciled with their comparatively lackadaisical, lackluster performance as HSE students? It seems appropriate at this point to summarize the interpretations of their behavior and attitudes supplied by teachers, fellow students over age thirty, counselors and support staff, as well as by the youngest students themselves. I will also offer some hunches (not hypotheses, just hunches) and conclude with some practical suggestions for programming.

Interpretations

From the Teachers' Perspective. For teachers, the increasing proportion of seventeen- to twenty-one-year-old participants was not an entirely welcome development. (Teachers were scrupulous in keeping their feelings to themselves, however, and few younger students were aware of — or seemed to worry about — teachers' opinions of them.) Many teachers expressed the view that the youngest students were repeating the behavior that they had displayed in the high schools they left: irregular attendance, passivity, and lack of "stick-to-itiveness." Two of the teachers also described a kind of magical thinking among very young adults, whereby they labored under the delusion that a more "positive attitude" toward schooling and a fierce desire to gain a diploma were sufficient for success. Teachers added dryly that both were necessary but not sufficient; hard work was also required, particularly of those without good reading and math skills.

Teachers also expressed the view that members of the age seventeen to twenty-one cohort are not "true" adults. Several teachers complained that, in effect "andragogy was wasted on the young" and that "the kids" did not appreciate their efforts to make the material interesting and relevant to the requirements of adult living. These efforts were clearly appreciated by students who were contemporaries of the teachers; by comparison, seventeen- to twenty-one-year-olds were less rewarding students, even when they were bright and successful.

From the Perspective of Older Students. Mature students viewed their seventeen- to twenty-one-year-old counterparts positively as laudable exceptions to school dropouts in general. In regard to the latter group, middle-aged students in particular expressed contempt and even fear of out-of-school youth. In contrast to the teachers, older students were generous in the distinctions they made between "kids" in general and "kids" in this program; like the teachers, however, they viewed the seventeen to twenty-one cohort as not yet fully adult. Older students expressed a thoughtful awareness of contemporary social influences on this age cohort and of the effect of these influences on behavior and attitudes. The life of the high school dropout today was perceived as more difficult than it had been even as few as ten years ago.

A number of students over age thirty expressed the view that for bright teenagers stuck in problem-ridden public high schools, dropping out was a "smart" (that is, rational) decision — or would have been, if the economy were not faltering and employers not so insistent on credentials. Accordingly, older students provided support and approval to the best and the brightest of the younger students, encouraging them in their ambitions for a college degree. However, very young students in the Adult Basic Education program were viewed as almost certain to fail in their attempts to gain a diploma and, therefore, were seen as potential "troublemakers."

From the Perspective of Counselors and Support Staff. Counselors, registrars, and people who did test scoring and record keeping described the seventeen to twenty-one-year-old students as immature perhaps but adults nonetheless. Counselors insisted that very young students are best served by being treated as adults capable of making their own decisions. Counselors described themselves as perplexed by the younger students' insistence on berating themselves for having dropped out of high school and pledging their determination to succeed. Counselors listened patiently and then cut short the self-criticism by saying, "Well, the point is you're here now, and this time you can make it. People with your placement test scores generally find..." One counselor remarked, "It's as if they can't go forward without a promise of absolution." One of the registrars interrupted, "Yes, and going back to school is their penance." The counselor acknowledged that the youngest students seem to exhibit little joy in returning to the classroom, and then he continued with his original theme; students twenty-one and under, he thought, feel a pressing need to put their high school years behind them and divest themselves of the emotional baggage of a troubled adolescence.

From the Younger Students' Perspective on Themselves. Younger students readily agreed with negative characterizations of their classroom behavior but insisted that little of it mattered. Many felt they could succeed without attending every class or diligently completing every assignment—in other words, by doing just enough to get by. Seventeen to twenty-one-year-olds were, of all the students, the most cynical about high school equivalency as an educational activity, viewing it as test preparation pure and simple. (At an emotional level, however, high school equivalency seemed to represent an important rite of passage). And, in fact, the best readers in this age group were able to "get by" with very little effort. However, students with less solid skills were not well served by their nonchalance.

For all their nonchalance, the seventeen to twenty-one-year-olds admitted considerable anxiety. They were most anxious about passing the GED, and their assessment of their chances often seemed to fluctuate with their moods. Asked about their other anxieties, they described the developmental tasks typically confronting their age cohort: "A good job, settling down, becoming my own grown-up person." Invited to compare the worries of his age group with those of older students in his classes, one young man stated: "they're 'together' people. I'm not. They're cute. They really care about being good students." And, indeed, the propensity of older students to start out simply to pass the test and then, catching fire as learners, to seek knowledge for its own sake gratified their teachers enormously. Few of the younger students ever caught fire.

The young students seemed pleased to be in classes with older adults, some of whom were parents' contemporaries. Most rejected the notion of grouping classes by age. One student stated, "They [older students] make the program seem less like high school." This sentiment was also echoed by teachers. One disgruntled instructor put it slightly differently, however: "Older students save the program from turning into a high school annex." Most of the youngest students were grateful for the encouragement and reassurance given them by older students, and they admired—although, for the most part, they did not emulate—their elders' matter-of-fact perseverance.

From the Researcher's Perspective. For me as researcher, a salient, provoking issue was the meaning of "adult." There was disagreement among different participant groups in this case study as to whether seventeen- to twenty-one-year-olds were immature adults, mature adolescents, or "teenyboppers." It was never clear to me exactly how the seventeen to twenty-one-year-olds identified their age reference group. On the one hand, they referred to themselves as "kids." On the other, they seemed anxious to put their high school years and their adolescence firmly behind them.

The meaning of "adult" is not simply a definitional quibble. Interwoven with one's perception of what it means to be an adult are expectations of appropriate adult behavior. Teachers, for instance, seemed to feel that students over thirty — their contemporaries — set the standard for adult students, and in a sense they resented the younger students for not meeting or conforming to that standard. Counselors insisted on treating younger students as if they were mature adults, despite considerable evidence to the contrary. The fact that almost all of these part-time teachers and counselors were employed in the day schools may have prompted in them a kind of dichotomous thinking. That dichotomy is between children and adults: You are either one or the other. In this regard, Cross (1981) criticizes Knowles's (1980) theory of andragogy because it defines learners as either children or adults. She proposes instead that age-associated differences among learners be conceptualized along developmental continua: physical, psychological, and sociocultural.

As Darkenwald explains in the second chapter of this volume, age categories employed by the National Center for Education Statistics (NCES) reflect the continuous nature of adult psychosocial development. NCES analyses distinguish between Stage 1 of young adulthood (ages seventeen to twenty-one) and Stage 2 (twenty-five to thirty-four). This case study supports the validity of such distinctions in educational programs serving a mixed-age clientele.

Recommendations

1. The value of screening, educational counseling, and differentiated instructional placement is clear, even though many high school equivalency programs lack the resources to mount a sophisticated effort. However, any HSE program experiencing an influx of very young, recent dropouts might consider providing group counseling especially for these students. Age-segregated instruction would not be desirable in a program like Garden's, where an age mix in classes seemed to benefit younger students at no cost to older students. However, Garden's young students are atypical regarding reading ability and motivation. Programs that serve young dropouts who are less advantaged and motivated and whose behavior is disruptive should consider age-segregated instruction if only to ensure continued participation by more mature adults.

2. Alerted by the comments of older student respondents, I believe that the higher attrition and lower perseverance displayed by even the most able and ambitious of the seventeen- to twenty-one-year-olds in Garden's HSE program may be accentuated among lower-level basic education (ABE) students in this age group. Local program

staff members are almost certainly aware of the special problems of young ABE students; decision makers at state and federal levels may not yet share this awareness. Practitioners should consider carefully the pros and cons of age-segregted instruction for this group of young learners.

3. Staff development activities should squarely address the issues raised by an increase in the enrollment of very young adults. At the very least, the air might be cleared and "ageist" stereotyping discouraged. Teachers and counselors could be encouraged to distinguish between different stages of adulthood and try to address the distinctive concerns of each. Also, though few HSE programs are able to provide supplementary instruction in job seeking and preparing for college, they might encourage enrollment in noncredit courses addressing these concerns where such courses are available in public school or community college continuing education programs.

4. Local program staff, professional associations, and state education department personnel should try to ensure that young dropouts and high school guidance counselors are aware of the academic requirements of the GED test and of the fact that it is not a substitute for a high school education. "Dumping" should be discouraged. Clearly, continuing educators incur some risks in promoting high school equivalency's cost effectiveness. "Cost-conscious legislators" (Lant, 1977) could encourage "dumping," transforming high school equivalency into just another track to a high school diploma. In my opinion, this very real threat should be strongly resisted. Most young dropouts require more than any high school equivalency program, not matter how comprehensive and successful, is able to provide.

References

Carnegie Council on Policy Studies in Higher Education. *Giving Youth a Better Chance: Options for Education, Work, and Service.* San Francisco: Jossey-Bass, 1980.

Cross, K. P. *Adults as Learners: Increasing Participation and Facilitating Learning.* San Francisco: Jossey-Bass, 1981.

General Educational Development Testing Service. *The GED Annual Statistical Report (1982).* Washington, D.C.: American Council on Education, 1982.

Grede, J., and Friedlander, J. *Adult Basic Education in Community Colleges.* ERIC Junior College Resource Review. Los Angeles: ERIC Clearinghouse for Junior Colleges, 1981.

Knowles, M. S. *The Modern Practice of Adult Education.* (Revised edition). Chicago: Follett, 1980.

Lant, J. K. "New Age Limits for State High School Equivalency Tests." *Phi Delta Kappan,* 1977, *59,* 54–55.

Larson, G. A. *Technical Specifications for an Alternative Test of High School Equivalency.* New Brunswick, N.J.: Center for Adult Development, Rutgers University, 1982.

Malizio, A. G., and Whitney, D. R. *Who Takes the GED Tests?* Washington, D.C.: American Council on Education, 1981.

Muraskin, L., and Fischer, J. K. "Adult Secondary Education: The State of the Art in GED Preparation and Credit Programs." Unpublished manuscript, Rutgers University, Graduate School of Education, 1975.

National Association for Public Continuing Adult Education. *1982 Public and Continuing Adult Education Almanac.* Washington, D.C.: National Association for Public Continuing Adult Education, 1982.

Franceska B. Smith works as a consultant in continuing education. She earned her doctorate in higher and adult education from Columbia University.

Programming for young parents should be responsive to the unique demands of role performance at this developmental stage.

Hospital-Based Programs for Young Parents

Carol E. Peterson

Young adulthood is the developmental period from the late teens to the early thirties. The developmental tasks of this period, according to Erikson (1980), relate to the issues of intimacy versus isolation and generativity versus stagnation. The second task, generativity, includes procreativity, productivity, and creativity — the generation of life, products, and ideas. Procreativity, as one manifestation of generativity, is the developmental task of establishing the adult-parent identity in the role of parent.

As a milestone in adult life, parenthood demarcates a transition between youth and adulthood. In Levinson and others (1978), parenthood signifies a choice in role and defines a place in the adult world. Knox (1977) indicates parenthood is typically initiated during the young-adult stage, with the majority of childbearing ending about age thirty. Parenthood, as a transition, acts as a prompt with adults, it causes them to review the past, undergo self-assessment and think about the future (Lowenthal and others, 1975). Permanent changes in our sense of self occur at this "watershed" in our adult life (Boston Women's Health Book Collective, 1978).

Parenthood in Relation to Other Roles of the Young Adult

Young adults engage in parenthood along with other roles, including those associated with marriage and work, and the parent function needs to be

G. G. Darkenwald, A. B. Knox (Eds.). *Meeting Educational Needs of Young Adults.* New Directions for Continuing Education, no. 21. San Francisco: Jossey-Bass, March 1984.

examined in relation to these roles. As a dynamic ever-changing state, parenthood interfaces with other milestones characterizing the tasks of the young-adult period — marriage and occupation. Parenthood typically follows them in the family life cycle and the course of adult development. Consideration of marriage and occupational roles when looking at parenthood underscores the fact that young adults perform a multiplicity of roles, with each role demanding certain levels of performance and integration with other roles.

Marriage. Parenthood causes a role shift in married couples, changing the husband-wife relationship by necessitating adjustments between spouses and between parent and child (Kimmel, 1974). Reappraisal of the spouse relationship may occur when marriage goes from dyad to family triad (Bischof, 1976).

Occupation. The onset of parenthood often occurs when marriage choices have been made and when the young adult accepts other adult responsibilities in the selection of a vocation and commitment to an occupational role. Occupational roles require a significant investment of time, challenging parents as they attempt to integrate the roles of parent and worker.

Impact of Role Relationships on Parent Education. Striking a balance among occupation, marriage, and parenthood becomes a challenging task for the young adult. In addition to the interface parenthood requires with other roles and individuals, changes at an individual level in self-concept and motivation, along with reworking unresolved childhood conflicts, often occur with the onset of parenthood (Kimmel, 1974). Timing, as Levinson and others (1978) have noted, is key to the nature of the parenthood experience — where it falls in the adult life span has special implications for the degree and quality of adaptation required. Parenting a newborn in young adulthood is qualitatively different from parenting in middle life. This is why an understanding of adult development and especially of developmental tasks is so important for program planning for young parents. Responsive continuing education programs on parenting for young adults have taken into account the unique characteristics, developmental tasks, and learning needs of this population. Education thus assists young adults in the performance of roles based upon developmental tasks where the timing of learning has special significance.

The family life cycle closely parallels adult development because the milestones relating to family events are considered marker events of the adult life span. Marriage and the birth of the first child, for example, are developmental milestones of the young-adult period of human development. They also represent the first two stages of family development. Because the family is the social context for parenthood, the study of family development helps continuing educators understand the developmental needs of young adults as parents relating to other life circumstances and to other individuals. In other words, practitioners can gain understanding of parent learning needs by understanding the reciprocal relationship between family roles and other adult roles.

Need for Parent Education for the Young Adult

A brother and sister constantly fight and argue with one another, causing a parent to wonder if they ever will have a close relationship as family members. A mother suspects her daughter is sexually active and deliberates about whether to discuss or ignore the issue. A young boy will not initiate or complete his homework without constant parental admonitions and close supervision. A disoriented and lethargic girl with poor school performance is questioned by parents about drug use. Sibling rivalry, sexual behavior, avoidance of responsibility, and drug abuse are familiar problems confronting young parents and challenging their abilities to manage the parent role effectively.

Inexperience and a lack of training in parenting contribute to the stress from these challenging situations and add to the irony that so little emphasis is given to preparation for a role that has such important long-range implications. The stress accompanying the parent role and the deficits in young adults' knowledge and skills create a need for educational intervention. Because most parents have romanticized notions and unrealistic expectations of parenthood, assisting couples and single parents in developing a realistic and knowledgeable picture of the parenting experience can aid in the transition (Kimmel, 1974).

During a child's early years, the manner in which parents relate to the child has a bearing on his or her subsequent development. These long-range implications make a parent's need for learning and readiness to learn all the more significant, and, in fact, becoming a parent is a life event that often spurs adults to seek information and engage in learning (Knox, 1977). Continuing educators and health care practitioners can offer programs aimed at meeting these needs (and at providing primary prevention before a problem occurs), thus improving the quality of the parent-child relationship.

Purpose of Parent Education

The purpose of parent education is to develop knowledgeable parents capable of making informed decisions about parenting practice and the health and welfare of their children. According to Fine (1980, p. xiii), parent education provides "exposure to ideas and skills about parenting, along with opportunities to ventilate and share feelings and experiences, [thus holding] the promise of facilitating healthy parenting." Goals for parent education consistent with the needs of parents and the nature of their problems generally include: helping parents toward greater self-awareness, helping with effective discipline, increasing parent-child communication, encouraging family fun, and transmitting useful information on child development.

While there exists increased interest in parent education programs, severe deficits in parenting skills exist. Potentially, parent education programs will increase the number of children being raised under better circumstances.

The possibility of achieving this goal increases as the number and variety of providers of parent education increases; in fact, this type of continuing education is becoming so prevalent that Fine (1980) and others assert that a parent education "movement" is developing.

Hospitals as Providers of Parent Education

University Hospital and Clinics, located in Madison, Wisconsin, offers health education programs for the community consistent with its mission to make health care resources accessible to its service area and population — Wisconsin and its citizens. Hospitals, indeed, are recognized by the American Hospital Association as appropriate institutions to offer health education programming for the public (American Hospital Association, 1975).

Continuing education and training for parents is a logical service for a hospital to provide because: (1) the latest advances in pediatric and teenage health care are available from medical experts, such as physicians, nurses, social workers, psychiatrists, and other medical personnel; (2) hospitals have credibility as sources of health information and services in the public's view, thus helping to encourage adult participation in educational programs; and (3) affiliation with a medical school, as is the case at the University of Wisconsin, results in an emphasis on education and research that benefits the program in the scope of services and of current information available on particular subjects.

Case Study: A Parent Education Program

For two consecutive years, University Hospital and Clinics has provided conferences on pediatric health care and parent education that are called "Pediatric Health Care in the '80s." This section describes the program, the process, and the rationale used in developing the conference. Special attention is given to illustrating how the program is responsive to the particular learning needs of young parents.

The first pediatric conference was held in 1982 as part of the hospital's community outreach programming. It consisted of a half-day program covering accidents, career and family, family as the patient, infections from daycare centers, drug abuse in teenagers, child abuse, pediatric illnesses, and sexuality. Eight topics were offered in two tracks, allowing parents to participate in four sessions of one track. The conference was held on a Saturday morning, lecture was the method used, and childcare was provided on site.

The second pediatric conference was held in 1983. The features of this conference are described here within the framework of the program's development — from needs assessment, program objectives, program format, content, methods, program services, and program implementation to evaluation. Developmental characteristics of the young adult will be cited as they pertain to program development considerations.

Needs Assessment. For both conferences, the Parents' Committee of the General Pediatric and Teenage Clinic served as the planning committee overseeing conference development. Parents from the hospital's service area, medical staff from the clinic, and hospital staff from administration and the Department of Training and Education comprised the committee's membership. Parental concerns relating to child-parent relationships and parenting practices were voiced by the parents; medical staff shared insights about health problems seen in their practice; and hospital staff provided information gleaned from their experience and a literature search on child development and parent education. The advice of child development experts was another source of guidance.

Concerns and needs were screened and prioritized based upon several criteria: (1) the value of education as a primary prevention for the identified problems; (2) the worth of education as a remedial solution for problems already manifested; (3) opinions of medical experts about the relative significance of a problem by frequency and degree of disability; (4) interests of the medical staff; (5) health care expertise available to address these subjects; and (6) guidance from the hospital's administration regarding allocation of resources for specific programs.

As a programming practice, practitioners should elicit the perceptions of educational need from the potential participants. Parents are a valid source of information for needs-assessment purposes, and their ideas should weigh equally with other expert sources. It is important to the program not to discount or neglect the target population's worth as a source for needs assessment.

Goals. Goals for the second conference specified the desirable outcomes for the program. The committee, clinic, and hospital aimed to: (1) make resources accessible to the community; (2) establish the hospital as a source of health information and expertise; (3) prevent problems that consume health care resources; (4) help parents develop confidence in parenting skills and practices; (5) provide information about medical and other services available to assist parents and children; and (6) create a positive association between education and the adaptation required in parenthood. Instructional objectives that addressed these goals were developed for the individual sessions.

Program Format. Because the previous conference's format was somewhat restrictive by requiring participants to select one of two multi-topic tracks, a format for the second conference was chosen to allow participants maximum freedom of choice based upon their personal preferences. Seven topics were offered concurrently and repeated in a second session. A second set of seven topics was also offered in this pattern. Participants chose four forty-five-minute sessions from fourteen. Consistent with principles of continuing education practice, learners were able to select those sessions having the most practical value for them.

Topics. Topics were based on the needs assessment results and program objectives. Included were: eating disorders, drug abuse, sexual abuse of children, sports medicine topics, learning styles of exceptional children (ages

three to eleven), physical development in adolescence, careers and parenthood, single parenting, parenting styles, behavioral management of children,
trials and tribulations of normal adolescence, and immunization decisions.
The following discussion of two of these topics illustrates the decision-making
criteria for topic selection.

Single Parenting. Four out of ten children spend part of childhood in one-
parent families, usually with the mother heading the household (Marr and
Kennedy, 1980). Traditional families undergo stress, but single-parent families are faced with even greater difficulties. Divorce, as a causal factor, rises
dramatically during the first years of marriage, reaching a peak at two to four
years into the marriage (Kimmel, 1974). Since most divorces occur within the
first years of marriage, young adults are sometimes faced with single-parent
situations soon after becoming parents.

Many problems of single parenthood are well documented: Parents are
required to share parent identities with parents from other periods in the
child's life. Parents and children have difficulties relating to stereotypes and
social expectations of the community. The single parent experiences increased
responsibility while support is absent. It is difficult to confer with the absent
parent on childrearing decisions and difficult to provide adequate relationship
experiences for the child with the absent parent (Marr and Kennedy, 1980).

Several factors contributed to the selection of single parenting as a conference topic. Because society is oriented toward the nuclear family, education
is needed to help families understand the normalcy of this atypical family
structure. The inordinate amount of stress these families experience provides
an additional reason to educate single parents about coping techniques. Dra-
matic increases in the number of single-parent situations warrant an emphasis
on this topic for a conference on parenting and child health issues.

Child Abuse. Child abuse is increasing, affecting more children and
severely inhibiting their growth and development (Karpowitz, 1980). Child
abuse includes physical abuse, neglect, and sexual molestation (Fried and
Holt, 1980).

Parents who abuse children typically repeat the negative parenting they
themselves experienced as children. Abusive behavior is more prevalent
among certain parents: teenage parents, unwed mothers, parents confused or
anxious about parenthood, young mothers having been subjected to poor parenting, and mothers with disturbed feelings about themselves as parents (Fine,
1980). Child abuse is also likely to occur where there is a lack of understanding
about normal development and of ability to deal with a developing child (Marr
and Kennedy, 1980). Violence as a social condition and crisis from loss of a
job or death are additional causes (Fried and Holt, 1980).

Parent education is a prevention strategy for child abuse that merits
support because of the increasing prevalence of the problem and its severe
consequences — the injuries and deaths that result (Lane, 1975). Because child
abuse occurs more frequently and is more violent among young-adult parents,

it has special significance for programming for this population (Fried and Holt, 1980).

Methods. Several considerations and criteria guided selection of methods that were compatible with the program's content and objectives. Lane's (1975, pp. 9–10) "Qualities of Relation" for reducing parenting stress served as general guidelines: "Parents need to feel accepted," "parents need to build identification with others who have like problems," and "parents need someone who will listen with an empathetic ear." Dialogues with parents revealed ideas about approaches to learning in particular content areas. Parents especially wanted to learn in ways that would facilitate applying practical information to their own circumstances.

The principle that adults learn best when instructional methods are varied and encourage participation was emphasized. Parents were encouraged to share problems in parenting and solutions they found useful with other parents dealing with similar situations. The notion that parents should look to one another as resources for parenting was stressed throughout the conference. Group methods in general were judged particularly suited for parent education because parents need the support of one another, the exchange of parenting solutions, and the reinforcing feeling that lets them know that they are not alone. Case examples and discussion were utilized in part because they are a favored method of learning by parents (Wycoff, 1980).

The Single Parenting session provides an example of decision-making regarding method selection. For single parents, it is important to discuss feelings related to loss because most single-parent situations derive from divorce, death, or abandonment. The case-study method was used to focus the discussion and create a climate for sharing experiences. Issues like finances, solo decision making, and managing increased responsibility were addressed. Belief systems were explored in relation to the "atypical" family stereotype that plagues single parents. Through active dialogue, parents discovered ways to adapt and manage their unique problems as they realized the increasing normalcy of their family form.

Program Services. Childcare is a consideration in developing parent education programs for young adults. Because their children are younger and require supervision, lack of childcare services acts as a barrier to participation for young parents. Offering childcare is expensive and involves a time investment of qualified staff, compliance with childcare regulations, insurance considerations, materials, and facilities. Practitioners should realize that childcare can constrain the program format by using program facilities. However, childcare expenses can be offset by program fees and may be warranted in light of higher enrollments (Wycoff, 1980).

Both conferences offered childcare because it was perceived that benefits outweighed constraints and costs. Based upon first-year childcare costs, second-year costs were considered in setting the program fee. Expenses were monitored to make judgments in the future about the cost-benefit ratio.

Program Implementation. Parent educators recommend scheduling programs to avoid summer, holidays, and weekdays. Weekends are optimal times to offer programming for this target group (Wycoff, 1980). Schedules should reflect concern and sensitivity for family and employment responsibilities. Saturdays were selected for both programs to allow employed parents to attend and to encourage spouses to participate. Having both parents receive information reduces the dissonance of disparate views on parenting practices.

Attrition rates between registration and actual program attendance were reduced for the second conference by a $5 registration fee to defray costs of providing childcare. Fees were kept low to encourage parents to participate. Young adults are at their lowest earning potential, and single parents often are financially burdened. To further encourage participation, the program offered free parking. Practitioners should consider these and other barriers to participation for young adults in planning continuing education programs.

Speakers were chosen based upon criteria advocated for speaker selection in continuing education programs—for example, high motivation, interest in new methods of teaching, and ability to treat learners like adults (Martin, 1982). Other factors, such as expertise and interest in subject matter, played a part in the decision.

A variety of medical specialties were represented by the speakers: pediatric and adolescent medicine, nursing, social work, and psychiatry. The Parents' Committee recommendations influenced speaker selection because many speakers were primary-care physicians for children of committee members. Other advisers on speaker selection were hospital administrators and pediatricians from the clinic.

In an effort to fine-tune publicity strategies and reach the young-parent audience, a plan was devised for maximum exposure at minimum cost. Direct mailings and radio and newspaper advertising were methods employed for program promotion. The direct-mail campaign included program announcements mailed to previous conference participants, participants attending previous health education programs, and parents of clinic patients served during the previous four years. Youth-serving organizations, area health and social service agencies, and local businesses serving parents received letters of invitation with program information. Program brochures were mailed to zip code areas having 30 percent or more of households with children. Census tract data provided the source for this information.

Radio announcements were aired on area stations with young-adult audiences. Program announcements were conducted for several days giving a program overview and ways to obtain registration information. The effectiveness of each promotional method was assessed by including in the evaluation questionnaire an item on how participants heard about the program.

Evaluation. Consumer satisfaction surveys about program quality and services were conducted the first year at the conference's conclusion. Participant satisfaction, cost effectiveness, and application of information to the learner's own situation were assessed in the second. Avoiding the "train and hope" pitfall of some programs, the second conference assessed the program's value in terms of impact on the lives of the parents attending (Wycoff, 1980). Participant satisfaction information is useful for certain decisions. For example, format changes the second year reflected a need to alter the previous year's format based upon participant reactions. Cost-effectiveness data provide information for decision making regarding fees, services, and promotion. And knowing if parents felt they could apply program information helps assess the value of methods designed to promote changes in attitudes, skills, and behavior.

Evaluation of this type can establish a cause-effect relationship between parent-child relationships and parent learning (Kaplan, 1980). In this manner, the program's degree of responsiveness to the needs of young adults can be gauged. If the concepts discussed in program sessions are applied in the parents' lives, then the provider can make informed judgments of a program's worth. For example, the amelioration of guilt feelings in women about dual role performance and the ability to cope with separation from the child are both issues for working mothers, and they relate to the value of the Career and Parenthood session. Similarly, participant suggestions for improvement of childcare services can be used as inputs in planning future childcare services. Knowledge of the recruitment media that brought in the most participants can help develop future promotion plans. These are examples of the value of evaluation for program improvement decisions.

Parent Education Needs and Program Suggestions

This case example depicts how young parents' needs can be addressed in a responsive fashion in a parent education program. The literature on parenting also contains suggestions for practitioners interested in programming for this audience. A sampling of these ideas is provided here.

According to Karpowitz (1980), information is sorely needed for the reconstituted family because of the severe developmental stress that this type of family undergoes. As this family type becomes more commonplace with increases in divorce and remarriage, the need for education becomes more apparent to assist family members in making the necessary adaptations and adjustments. Issues such as stepchildren's preferences for one parent, children's feelings of discrimination, and competition among stepchildren constitute stressful situations for these families.

Education about the stages of family life, as Karpowitz advocates, helps parents anticipate points of crisis and potentially challenging situations. Parents can learn about developmental issues related to family roles, preparing them for the role performance required. An understanding of the family life cycle facilitates adaptation to the developmental transitions that the family experiences.

Parents lack the knowledge and skills, Marr and Kennedy (1980) point out, that enable access to community resources. Understanding the complex network of youth- and parent-serving agencies and resources is important for parents and can be developed through parent education programs.

Parents who are uninformed about child development tend to make excessive demands of their children. Wycoff (1980) suggests that programs focused on the development of preschool-aged children can help parents avoid unrealistic expectations and promote better child-parent relationships.

Marr and Kennedy (1980) indicate that adoptive parents can benefit from information that assists them in dealing with separation-loss issues, and foster families can benefit from problem-solving and support groups. Interventions are needed to help such families attain skills in conflict resolution and stress management.

Summary

Parents are experts when it comes to knowledge of their children. They invest significant amounts of time, emotional energy, and resources in their lifelong commitment to childrearing and parenting. Consequently, continuing educators should consider parents as authorities on children.

Practitioners should also consider the body of literature on adult development, parenting, and adult education as a resource for the development of responsive parent education programs. As Knox (1977, p. 157) has observed, "Practitioners can use developmental generalizations about adult performance to anticipate both likely adult life cycle changes and the typical needs for learning and adaptation associated with these change events."

Parent education programs are an investment in the future. Practitioners developing responsive programs for young parents prevent problems from developing and assist in adaptation as problems occur. There is no other acceptable alternative. Pringle (1980) cautions:

> Failure to provide the necessary services and the programs for children and their families merely postpones the day when society has to pay a much higher price for not willing the means earlier. In the long run, the cost is extremely high—not only in terms of human misery and wasted potentialities but also in terms of unemployability, mental ill-health, crime, and a renewed cycle of inadequate parenting. Even in the short run, it is by no means economic to do too little and do it too late [p. 31].

References

American Hospital Association. "Statement on Health Education: Role and Responsibility of Health Care Institutions." Chicago: American Hospital Association, 1975.

Bischof, L. *Adult Psychology.* New York: Harper & Row, 1976.

Boston Women's Health Book Collective. *Ourselves and Our Children.* New York: Random House, 1978.

Erikson, E. "Elements of a Psychoanalytic Theory of Psychosocial Development." In S. I. Greenspan and G. H. Pollock (Eds.), *Infancy and Early Childhood, the Course of Life: Psychoanalytic Contributions Toward Understanding Personality Development.* Vol. 1. Rockville, Md.: National Institute of Mental Health, 1980.

Fine, M. "The Parent Education Movement: An Introduction." In M. Fine (Ed.), *Handbook on Parent Education.* New York: Academic Press, 1980.

Fried, S., and Holt, P. "Parent Education: One Strategy for the Prevention of Child Abuse." In M. Fine (Ed.), *Handbook on Parent Education.* New York: Academic Press, 1980.

Kaplan, M. "Evaluating Parent Education Programs." In M. Fine (Ed.), *Handbook on Parent Education.* New York: Academic Press, 1980.

Karpowitz, D. "A Conceptualization of the American Family." In M. Fine (Ed.), *Handbook on Parent Education.* New York: Academic Press, 1980.

Kimmel, D. *Adulthood and Aging: An Interdisciplinary, Developmental View.* New York: Wiley, 1974.

Knox, A. B. *Adult Development and Learning: A Handbook on Individual Growth and Competence in the Adult Years.* San Francisco: Jossey-Bass, 1977.

Lane, M. *Education for Parenting.* Washington, D.C.: National Association for Education of Young Children, 1975.

Levinson, D., Darrow, C. N., Klein, E. B., Levinson, M. H., and Braxton, M. *The Seasons of a Man's Life.* New York: Knopf, 1978.

Lowenthal, M. F., Thurnher, M., Chiriboga, D., and Associates. *Four Stages of Life: A Comparative Study of Women and Men Facing Transitions.* San Francisco: Jossey-Bass, 1975.

Marr, P., and Kennedy, C. "Parenting Atypical Families." In M. Fine (Ed.), *Handbook on Parent Education.* New York: Academic Press, 1980.

Martin, M. "Be a Better Teacher." In C. Klevins (Ed.), *Materials and Methods in Adult and Continuing Education.* Los Angeles: Klevens, 1982.

Pringle, M. *A Fairer Future for Children: Towards Better Parenting and Professional Care.* London: Macmillan, 1980.

Wycoff, J. "Parent Education Programs: Ready, Set, Go." In M. Fine (Ed.), *Handbook on Parent Education.* New York: Academic Press, 1980.

Carol E. Peterson is coordinator of Community Health Education at University Hospital and Clinics, Madison, Wisconsin. She has also served as coordinator for the health education outreach program in a community hospital. She received her master's degree in Continuing and Vocational Education at the University of Wisconsin–Madison.

*Business and industry use a variety of approaches to develop
effective young managers. However, the needs of organizations
and young managers are not always congruent*

Developing Young Managers

Pearl Greenstein

From age twenty-five to the early thirties is the time during which most young
men and women who want management careers in business and industry
begin their ascent. These young adults stress "interesting jobs, income, and
potential fame" as important to them (Knox, 1977, p. 215). Chickering and
Havighurst (1981) also describe this group as beginning or progressing up the
career ladder, seeking satisfaction, advancement, and economic rewards.
Levinson and others (1978, p. 22) have described this period as early adulthood, the time during which a man (or woman) is "struggling to establish his
place in society," "the time when he establishes himself first at a junior level
and then advances along some formal or informal ladder."

The literature is replete with descriptions of developmental needs and
career tasks for this age group, and there are many management career programs that ostensibly meet some of the life-stage needs of this group. However, initiation and implementation of such programs within industry have had
and still have less to do with the young employee's life cycle or developmental
needs than with the organization's needs. As Morgan, Hall, and Martier
(1979) point out, most career development programs in companies have been
initiated by top management to ensure a supply of talented personnel; in most
cases, organizational needs, rather than adult developmental needs, influence
the types of programming supported. For the company, career programs are
intended to assure such benefits as maximum contribution from individual
employees, reduction of underemployment, promotion from within, large
management pools, or improvement of performance and profitability.

G. G. Darkenwald, A. B. Knox (Eds.). *Meeting Educational Needs of Young Adults.* New Directions
for Continuing Education, no. 21. San Francisco: Jossey-Bass, March 1984. **67**

In the 1950s, for example, in a time of forecasted expansion, a large pool of trained executives was required but only a small group was available. Therefore, "fast-track" programs for promising young personnel were initiated. When these programs were developed, "whiz kids" like Robert McNamara took advantage of them. The idea was "to spot the talented individuals, give them brief stints at a variety of high-visibility jobs, and build a new generation of top managers fast" (Byrne and Konrad, 1983, p. 77).

In the mid 1980s there is still a need for talented young managers, but the forecasts for continued economic and company expansion have changed. In addition, organizations have found problems, such as the jealousy or demoralization of nonfast-track personnel, developed as a result of such programs. Thus, in many companies, the fast-track program has been modified or replaced with other kinds of management training. The organization's needs have changed, and so have programs for high-potential young managers. So, what happens now for the promising young manager in the corporate world? What kind of management career programming do organizations provide to meet their own needs and perhaps also the career development needs of young management employees?

Several approaches to general as well as management career development are currently used in American business and industry. They include the following: individual planning and counseling; use of formal assessment procedures for diagnosis and selection; provision of a career information service; special-population services (such as those for women or minorities); organizational career planning—that is, "foresightful planning for the future of the organization (rather than the individual) so that progress and change are thoughtfully engineered" (Eabon, 1982, p. 7); and training and development geared toward improving the knowledge and performance of employees both to increase present proficiency and to prepare them for upcoming jobs.

Some programs use elements of all of the above. However, most can be broadly categorized within the last two approaches, training and development or organizational planning. The development practices implemented by any one company depend upon available funding, location of the program within an organization (is it sponsored by a specific department or by personnel?), and upon the specific needs of the organization itself (Eabon, 1982).

The remainder of this chapter describes some of the programs that now exist for the young manager. Included is a discussion of how individuals are selected for and rewarded in these programs, as well as what problems and what positive outcomes result from the programming. Several brief examples of current programs and one case study of a high-risk, high-reward management development program are also included. Finally, we review some of the implications for continuing educators of the present kinds of programs for young managers.

Program Trends and Characteristics

When one considers management training and development as offered by industry, generally one cannot think in terms of a sequence of courses or experiences that one takes in order to get "to the end of the rainbow." Whatever the training format an organization adopts, it is clear that no promises are made, no guarantees offered to the young aspirant that at the end he or she will become a second- or third-level manager or higher executive. This is quite different from the rather obvious route of the university, where the right courses are pretty much known, exactly how to reach "success" (that is, graduation) is understood, and how long it will take can be easily calculated. In school, "the passage of time and status changes are clearly signaled by changes in routine and frequent vacations" (Morgan, 1980, p. 100). In industry, no such clear, regular signals of progress are built into the system for the young manager.

Some young entries have great difficulty in finding their way through this new system, where the cues may be less obvious and the time frame less defined than they experienced in school. Some succeed rapidly. Kellogg (1978) has described certain characteristics of young managers who rapidly achieve success in the business world, though they did not necessarily succeed within their earlier school world. These achievers tend to be loners who, in their younger years, were more comfortable with adults than with children their own age; they used their youth constructively and found out what they did not know and then found the right people to inform them; they had an eagerness to learn that separated them from average counterparts who were loath to admit mistakes; they were restless, which led to a striving that was unique among the early achievers; they also knew when a job was not for them and had the courage to leave and the ability to profit in some way from each job; and finally, for each, there was a willingness to work hard.

Whereas most companies used to have formal group orientations and lectures about the overall structure of the company, the emphasis in many places has now shifted to "what does the new person need to know to function appropriately in his or her particular job environment." Training is provided to the employee that is directly related to identified on-the-job needs. Primary emphasis is on the individual's work, how this work fits into his or her group, and how the group fits into the total organization. For example, line managers may attend a "train the trainer" course that covers aspects of learning and motivational theory; the managers can then apply this information to specific activities they have to carry out (*Staffing Systems...*, 1972).

Changes in learning format from general lecturing to participant involvement may serve both the restless, rapid succeeder and the more unsure but still high-potential young manager. They also relate to Knowles's (1980) view of adults as learners who do best when asked to use their experience and apply new knowledge to solve real-life problems.

Along with the trend from the general to the specific in content and goals, there is also greater variety in the kinds of programs available now for the aspiring young manager. Lower-level managers may be given an opportunity to participate in workshops lasting several hours to several days. These workshops may be offered by trainers employed by the company, by consultants, or local university faculty. Examples of typical subjects include time management, budget planning, leadership, decision making, conflict management, and career planning. Workshops for higher-level managers may focus on corporate strategy, organization design, productivity, and economic and political trends and their impact on the organization. Experts may be asked to present different views. Many universities offer executive development programs ranging from several weeks to a year. Some organizations offer sequences of training courses. Individuals may take part in different training sequences at different stages of their careers. One course or workshop builds on what was learned in previous training experiences. Sometimes employee development is less formal—for example, second-level managers may give feedback or direction to first-level managers or act as role models.

Training in technical and managerial skills represents a large financial investment for a company. It is a useful investment only if those trained spend much of their careers in the organization. The most extensive training programs are likely to be offered by "long-term" employers rather than employers who experience rapid turnover. In some companies, "new employees are expected to spend their working lives in the firm and regularly go through intensive training programs to upgrade their skills" (*Staffing Systems...*, 1972, p. 16).

As we mentioned earlier, programs may serve many purposes for the company. The sections that follow describe three types of career programs available to aspiring young managers. Each program helps to develop young managers, but each serves a different company-defined goal. First is an example of a slow-growth program for newly recruited employees who are potential managers. Second is a program to create from within the company a pool of executive talent. Third is a program designed specifically to recruit and rapidly develop young managers who can bring new ideas and leadership styles to executive positions.

External Recruitment: Integrated Development Model

A development program in a division of a large communications firm combines early group orientation with a combination of on-the-job and classroom learning experiences. All entry-level professional employees, whether high potential or "average," go through a two-year introductory program. No one is overtly labeled as "fast track." All are placed for the first six weeks in an orientation program to learn about company policies and products.

During the two years, there is a combination of work experience and company schooling. The new employee services accounts, increases technical expertise, and learns management techniques. Only after these learning and on-the-job experiences can the employee move up to what would be a first management job in which he or she is responsible for others.

In this type of program, the individual can be observed, given increased responsibility, and rewarded by being selected for special advanced training. Many courses on communication and leadership skills, financial management, and technical subjects are available. This type of program allows both the potential young manager and the company time to make decisions.

Internal Recruitment: Integrated Development Model

One of the major reasons given by employers for management development programs is to facilitate promotion from within the corporation. This allows young managers to have somewhere to go within the company. The Management Readiness Program at Merrill Lynch is an example of this kind of developmental program. The program combines many elements mentioned earlier—career counseling by career development professionals, an inventory of participants' skills, management development courses, skills training, and special attention to the needs of women and minorities.

The program begins with a three-day seminar covering self-assessment, organizational norms, and introduction to senior management. All participants are assigned to groups of four, and each "development quartet" is assigned a mentor. This person, who is a department head or other higher level manager, serve as a counselor/adviser during the six months of the program. The group meets at least once a month, and the mentor gives advice about the culture of the corporation and assists participants in meeting individual goals. Application for participation in the program is initiated by the individual and his or her immediate manager. The career development administrator selects thirty-two participants based on the manager's recommendation and the participant's application.

During the three-day orientation period, participants must begin a personal development plan that is put into more complete form by the end of about three weeks. Participants are then expected to begin to carry out their developmental activities. Three classroom courses are offered—business writing, effective presentations skills, and selection interviewing. In addition, there are a number of computer-based management courses in the curriculum, including managerial success, time management, and issues and perspectives in management.

This program is intended to broaden employees' understanding about career choices and to assist them in building networks with peers, managers, and mentors. The program also gives the participants some important visibility to executives. Although there is no typical age for participants in this program, most are in their late twenties (Kaye and Farren, 1982; Pittari and Drake, 1983).

Another example of management development for young employees is the program at Union Carbide. The company offers several series of developmental programs tailored to specific classes of employees, including "Programs for Supervisors," "Programs for Managers," and "Programs for Executives." Although participation in each series is voluntary, attendance is based on an identified job-related need and requires departmental sponsorship. Program goals are to help individuals already doing an effective job do an even better job and to prepare individuals for future career growth within the company. All programs are designed to complement other forms of skill development, such as on-the-job training and attendance at university or other external programs.

Union Carbide's Corporate Management Development Unit offers a "Needs Analysis Guide" for each series of programs. Potential participants are instructed to discuss with their managers the areas that need development and subsequently to identify their strengths and weaknesses in a written career plan. They also are asked to seek feedback from peers who might help clarify the skills needing improvement. Once the skills to be improved are identified, individuals are directed to the "Needs Analysis Guide" to select the specific programs designed to meet these needs. There are a variety of programs available, including finance and accounting, time management, and productive conflict management.

Union Carbide puts responsibility for management development and growth partly on the individual, partly on the organization, and partly on the individual's supervisors. This sharing of responsibility, whether formalized as in the Merrill Lynch program or less formalized but still present as in this program, is typical of many development opportunities offered by companies.

External Recruitment: A Case Study of a Fast-Track Model

In 1976, a large Western-based communications company forecasted considerable growth but also rapid executive attrition within the company. The growth outlook exceeded the number of potential executives available, and therefore the company had to plan for rapid development of new management personnel. Because of predicted rapid growth and major changes in the technology of its industry, the company was looking for managers with a variety of backgrounds and who could move people from one point to another, who would be willing to take risks.

The candidates for this program tend to be in their early and mid twenties. Before being accepted, they have to undergo intensive assessment. Assessment includes, first, written general-ability tests. If these are passed, then the person goes to an interview in which the interviewer looks for such qualities as leadership, autonomy, and risk taking. Candidates who pass the interview phase next go to an all-day session in which they are assigned to a small group that participates in several role-playing and in-basket exercises. Four observers are present the entire day; their roles are to give directions, observe, and take notes. Two days after this session, participants are notified of acceptance or rejection. At the time of acceptance, an agreement is signed to the effect that the new employee understands that within one year after entry the company has the right to recommend termination from the program. They realize from the beginning that this is a high risk, high-reward program.

Once accepted into the program, participants immediately are given a first-level line-management position. They attend special technical training only if their immediate manager believes that it is necessary to their performance of the job. Early in this initial management assignment, they may also meet as a small group or as individuals with their program coordinator and receive some orientation. However, their primary mentor or link with company routine and policy is their immediate superior.

During this first-level management experience, they are observed both by their manager and by the program coordinator in order to ascertain their potential for getting their subordinates to perform and to be productive. Their value is not measured by how much they produce but by the performance of their subordinates. Participants know in advance the bases upon which they will be evaluated, including risk-taking behavior, growth, creativity, and innovation. They are evaluated formally four times a year, both in writing and verbally, with the immediate manager and the coordinator present. In addition, every six months the program participants who enter at the same time have a group meeting. Meeting format and content are decided by members of the group. The coordinator uses these meetings to observe leadership, originality, planning, resource allocation, sensitivity to upper management, assertiveness, and energy level.

There are no guarantees attendant with this program — only opportunities for high visibility and growth. Also, no new position is created for the people within the program; they must occupy, or be promoted to, existing vacancies.

To date, approximately ninety-seven people have been selected for the program. Of these, 50 percent did not complete it. About 40 of those who did not complete the program were asked to leave because the match was seen as inappropriate. The others left on their own for a variety of reasons. As part of this case study the program coordinator and three recent participants in the program were interviewed. Two recently had been promoted to second-level managers. The third had not yet received that promotion. All were under the age of thirty when they began the program, but the third was by far the youngest. All were asked the same questions: What were the positive aspects of the program for you? What were the negative aspects of the program? What major issues do you see for this kind of program?

Summary of Positive Responses. All three participants viewed "opportunity" as the greatest asset of the program. This included the opportunity to meet and get to know upper-level management, which gives participants great visibility. The participants felt that members of this special program "have doors opened" for them by virtue of their participation. In addition, opportunities to work on special projects are given because of the perception "that you can handle them." There also is the opportunity "to be able to associate with some of the brightest employees as your peers."

Other assets were mentioned by one or more of the interviewees: "In this program you are immediately given responsibility and held accountable";

"you are better off being identified as a risk taker than as a security-oriented person." The competitive aspects of the program also were seen as exciting and a positive force: "You are able to use your peers as a measure of your own progress because you respect them."

Summary of Negative Responses. The complaints about the program were more variable than the positive reactions: "Much of your success depends upon your immediate manager, and therefore more careful identification of a strong second-level manager is needed"; "you need someone who will act as a first mentor to the new management employee because this person is important to your understanding of the system"; "too much of the manager's success is left to luck or fate"; "the contract agreement led participants to believe that they would have more support than they had in reality"; "it is too difficult to get to the administrator of the program"; "when the program's administrator changes, the rules of the game change"; "a rotational job was promised, but that is not what happened."

Although the three had somewhat differing views on the positive and negative aspects of the program, all agreed that it was an exciting, though sometimes frustrating, opportunity and that they were pleased to be a part of it.

Summary of Results of the Program. The preceding case study provides an example of a fast-track program, and, according to staff and participants, it exemplifies many of the issues inherent in running such programs. For example, how does one deal with "regular-track" peers who are not among "the chosen"? Some peers, as well as immediate superiors, feel threatened by the participants. Some exhibit attitudes of "why did I slave all these years to be passed up by these people with no experience?" Some of the middle-level managers apparently do not understand the program and are not supportive. Participants in the program try to deal with these attitudes by working very hard in order to prove themselves.

The internal pressures on the participants to perform at extraordinary levels at all times sometimes block task completion—they cannot simply write a "good memo," for example; they must write a "great memo." There is the fear of failure and of not living up to the expectations of the program. Nevertheless, those who make it through what might be called a rather Darwinian program develop in a short period of time the skills needed both to negotiate the obstacles of the organization and to implement new management ideas and innovative, money-saving plans—which is what the company wanted to begin with.

Issues and Implications for the Practitioner

From the programs illustrated and the discussion surrounding them, several isues and implications seem apparent for the design of future programs for young managers. These include the importance of matching company and employee expectations and goals, of looking at changes in society as they affect program development and changes in the economy as they affect advancement opportunities and programs, and of using management programs for more than just training toward advancement.

One of the most important issues, both from the company's and the potential manager's view, is the program's "goodness of fit" between the individual's goals and needs and those of the company. When there is a match between these, both benefit. However, even in the rapid-development program, with its extensive preassessment process, there was a 50 percent attrition rate. Regardless of whether such programs are "slow" or "fast," they are costly.

Young graduates of the master's in business administration (MBA) programs come into the work place expecting positions of high satisfaction and rapid reward. If this is not what they find, they leave. High turnover among this group is not unusual. There appears, is some cases, to be a difference between some companies' views of roles for the new MBA and the university's promotion of the MBA. As a recent article on the topic put it, "Many companies, having concentrated their efforts on the courting process, give scant attention to the new MBAs continuing development within the organization" (Weldon and Weldon, 1981, p. 30).

Some companies have decided to deal with these issues by doing more upfront assessment as well as more exploration of employees' goals before investing in extensive training and development programs for young managers (Lancaster and Berne, 1981). Other companies try to deal with "matching" problems by not differentiating among young potential managers during their first year. This allows for orientation, observation, settling in, meaningful assignments, assessment, and demonstration of performance and potential. After that, some may be slotted for more rapid and extensive development (London and Stumpf, 1982).

Attitudinal, technological, and demographic changes in society raise problems to which company-sponsored training programs have to respond. For example, dual-career couples, changes in childrearing responsibilities, and desire for personal gratification make it less certain that an employee will automatically say yes to developmental programs that require moves or will even say yes to a promotion. Thus, the company may invest much money and time in a training program and not get the return that it wanted.

The educational level of young managers, as well as of executives, is increasing rapidly. As the literature indicates, those who have more education tend to participate more in continuing education. Advanced employees expect education as one of the "perks" of employment. However, extensive educational programs are very costly for the company.

Conversely, rapid technological changes make effective continuing training and development imperative for young managers in order to grow within their organization and to help the organization to grow. "Today a rising executive doesn't debate about whether to continue his formal education. He zeros in on how and when and where," says W. W. Clements, chairman of the Dr. Pepper Company (Broderick, 1980, p. 22).

Perhaps one of the ways to meet both the young manager's needs for education and the need for the company to get its money's worth is shared responsibility. In the Union Carbide and Merrill Lynch models, the company provided the opportunities for the young managers, but it was up to them to take the initiative for participation and the responsibility for following through. Some segment of each of these programs involved individualized learning modules. Perhaps this shared-responsibility model would not be appropriate for all employees, but certainly those who wish to be managers should demonstrate this type of motivation.

Training tends to increase expectations for promotion. However, when new positions are not available, there is no promotion. Instead, there may be employee dissatisfaction or attrition. Sometimes neither the company nor the individual is responsible for the discrepancy between the original promises and the eventual reality of a position. Changes in economic conditions or corporate growth patterns may not allow even high-potential people to rise as quickly as justified or as originally expected.

In the rapid-development program, promotion time went from an average of 24.5 months in the late seventies to 34 months at present. This change had nothing to do with participant quality but rather with company growth rate. To head off attrition and decrease disaffection, the coordinator raised the problem with these young high-potential managers. He talked with them individually, giving them assurances that the company still supported them and their promotion as early as would be feasible. So far, all managers have remained with the company.

How can management development programming respond to changes in growth and therefore in promotion patterns? Some have included in programming an attempt to change the attitude that "up" is the only way to career satisfaction. They stress alternative status and satisfaction routes, such as prestigious high-visibility assignments or elite educational opportunities.

In addition to trying to mold young managers' attitudes, companies also use programming as a way of "holding on to" bright young managers. Hall and Lerner (1980, pp. 433–434) point out that "with all the children of the postwar baby boom becoming firmly ensconced in middle age and with organizational funding resources becoming increasingly scarce, the need to effectively develop and utilize the talents of employees is urgent." Large companies, such as IBM, not only require initial training for young managers but also offer them at least forty additional hours of training each year. In 1982, IBM spent more than $500 million on employee education and training ("The Colossus That Works," 1983).

Whether or not company-sponsored management development programs play an important role in the careers of future generations of young managers depends upon how important businesses and industry perceive these programs to be to their economic health. Importance may be measured by such things as profit from an innovation that saved the company money, increased employee productivity, increased retention of valued young managers, the recruitment of high-potential managers in an increasingly competitive market, or an increased talent pool from which to draw upon for creativity. Whatever the measure, designing programs that meet the career development needs of this age group and that utilize appropriate adult learning techniques will have to be perceived by the company as valuable to meeting the company's own needs. The practitioner who wants to develop or manage such programs must keep these points in mind.

References

Broderick, M. "Continuing Education: Cutting Edge in Climbing the Career Ladder." *Marketing Times,* June 1980, pp. 21–24.
Byrne, J. A., and Konrad, W. "The Fast Track Slows Down." *Forbes,* July 18, 1983, pp. 77–78.
Chickering, A. W., and Havighurst, R. J. "The Life Cycle." In A. W. Chickering and Associates (Eds.), *The Modern American College: Responding to the New Realities of Diverse Students and a Changing Society.* San Francisco: Jossey-Bass, 1981.
"The Colossus That Works." *Time,* July 11, 1983, pp. 44–54.
Eabon, M. F. "Career Development in the Work Place." *Career Planning and Adult Development Journal,* Winter 1982, pp. 5–7.
Hall, D., and Lerner, P. "Career Development in Work Organizations: Research and Practice." *Professional Pscyhology,* 1980, *11,* 420–435.
Kaye, B. L., and Farren, C. "Management Readiness: A Program and Its Players." *Personnel,* 1982, *59,* 65–72.
Kellogg, M. A. *Fast Track: The Super Achievers and How They Make It to Early Success, Status, and Power.* New York: McGraw-Hill, 1978.
Knowles, M. S. *The Modern Practice of Adult Education.* Chicago: Follett, 1980.
Knox, A. B. *Adult Development and Learning: A Handbook on Individual Growth and Competence in the Adult Years.* San Francisco: Jossey-Bass, 1977.
Lancaster, A., and Berne, R. *Employer-Sponsored Career Development Programs.* Information Series No. 231. Columbus: The ERIC Clearinghouse on Adult, Career, and Vocational Education, National Center for Research in Vocational Education, Ohio State University, 1981. (ERIC Document Reproduction Service, no. ED 205 779.)
Levinson, D., Darrow, C. N., Klein, E. B., Levinson, M. H., and Braxton, M. *The Seasons of a Man's Life.* New York: Knopf, 1978.
London, M., and Stumpf, S. A. *Managing Careers.* Reading, Mass.: Addison-Wesley, 1982.
Morgan, M. A. *Managing Career Development.* New York: D. Von Nostrand, 1980.
Morgan, M., Hall, D., and Martier, A. "Career Development Strategies in Industry: Where Are We and Where Should We Be?" *Personnel,* 1979, *56,* 13–30.
Pittari, L., and Drake, D. "The Management Readiness Program: A Career Development Program That Works." *IAPW Journal,* Winter 1983, pp. 15–19.
Staffing Systems: Management and Professional Jobs. New York: Conference Board, 1972.
Weldon, T. D., and Weldon, N. R. "Meeting Expectations: New MBAs and Their Employers." *Business Horizons,* 1981, *24,* 30–34.

Pearl Greenstein is currently director of continuing professional education, Center for Adult Development, Rutgers University. She received her doctorate in continuing education from Rutgers University.

Basic skills education linked with job training provides an
effective strategy for reaching educationally alienated young adults.

Integrating Basic Skills
Education with Job Training

William J. Buckingham

Defining the Problem

The need for more basic skills training in the primary and secondary grades is supported by national and local studies that emphasize the need for individuals to be competent in basic reading and math skills to survive in an increasingly technological society. Many states have instituted "back-to-basics" programs and competency-based testing within their public school systems to assure that all high school graduates have mastered the basics.

The same studies have also expressed an alarming concern that a large number of young adults are functionally illiterate. A recent study entitled *Basic Skills in the U.S. Work Force* (Center for Public Resources, 1983) quotes the rate of illiteracy at 17 percent of white, 43 percent of black, and 56 percent of Hispanic seventeen-year-olds. In addition, the number of youth who annually drop out of the public schools is estimated between 700,000 (Center for Public Resources, 1983) and 1,000,000 (Novak and Dougherty, 1980).

This group of undereducated young adults imposes significant burdens and costs on society. A 1972 report from the Senate Committee on Equal Educational Opportunity (Jones, 1977) estimated the cost in 1969 for undereducated males between the ages of twenty-five and thirty-four to be $71 billion in

G. G. Darkenwald, A. B. Knox (Eds.). *Meeting Educational Needs of Young Adults.* New Directions
for Continuing Education, no. 21. San Francisco: Jossey-Bass, March 1984.

lost tax revenue and $3 billion in welfare expenditures. Apart from economic considerations, society pays a price in increased urban poverty and decreased social stability. "This lack of stability surfaces in all forms of crimes against property and persons" (Novak and Dougherty, 1979, p. 5). Dropouts are six to ten times more likely to be involved in crime than in-school youth (Jones, 1977), and an estimated 75 percent or more of inmates in state prisons are high school dropouts (Novak and Dougherty, 1979).

The impact on the private sector has only begun to be analyzed. The *Basic Skills in the U.S. Work Force* study concludes that there is a "significant problem of basic skill deficiencies among secondary school graduates and nongraduates entering the work force, from the perspective of business" (Center for Public Resources, 1983, p. 48). The report also identifies the following losses to business as a result of this skill deficiency problem: lost productivity, poor product quality, lost time for inaccurate work, increased management and supervision time, increased worker safety problems, and incurred expenses for remedial training programs. Although the financial loss to business has not been calculated, the report implies that most employers consider it significant.

The consequences to the individual for dropping out of school and for not having adequate literacy and computational skills can be devastating. Chances for securing employment, advancing in a career, and earning an adequate income are greatly reduced. These factors have a profound influence on an individual's job satisfaction and general quality of life.

Although some dropouts are able to secure permanent employment, the majority face severe barriers. Barriers include those imposed by society (for example, the stigma of being a dropout) and ones that are self-generating and are manifested through negative and often disruptive behaviors and attitudes. Many dropouts enter adult society with battered self-images and a hostility toward educational and social institutions. These individuals have been characterized as possessing most of the following attributes: a low self-concept, poor social adjustment, an inability to relate to authority figures, a lack of future orientation, and an inability to tolerate structured activities (Novak and Dougherty, 1979). Having faced repeated failures in school, dropouts generally consider themselves less knowledgeable than others and incapable of learning. Many are reluctant to risk exposing their lack of skills and refuse to become involved in activities that may remind them of the frustrations and embarrassments that they faced in school.

Many local communities address this situation by offering adult basic education classes for remedial literacy skills and high school completion. These programs generally attract individuals who are motivated to improve their lives and who recognize education as a way to do this. The problem is that these programs find it difficult to attract and keep individuals who are reluctant to return to an educational setting. The remainder of this chapter describes an alternative program in Madison, Wisconsin, that was specifically designed to work with young adults who had been labeled "unteachable." The first section gives an overview of this project's development and structure. The second section lists the factors that made this project successful in its orientation and approach to continuing education for young-adult dropouts.

Describing the Skills Center

Skills Center was a basic skills program operated by the Madison Area Technical College in conjunction with the Madison-Dane County Employment and Training Consortium. Established in the summer of 1973 under the then newly created Comprehensive Employment and Training Act (CETA), this program later became the hub of the CETA training network and delivery system in Dane County.

Originally, the Madison Area Technical College responded to a request from the staff of a community-based CETA job-training program to establish an individualized, alternative basic skills project. The CETA staff had decided that the training that some of their participants were receiving on various job sites was not enough to overcome their employability barriers. Many of the participants were recent high school dropouts (ages sixteen to twenty-two) who had also dropped out of alternative educational programs within and outside of the public school system. All had insufficient academic skills to compete in the job market. Both the Madison Area Technical College and this CETA job-training program agreed that these individuals were most in need of basic skills education but least likely to seek training on their own and that they would be more likely to participate if basic skills education was linked to their job training.

Skills Center opened with an enrollment of twenty students. Each student attended for two hours a day and spent the remainder of the day working on a job site. Participation at Skills Center was required if the student wanted to be in the CETA program. All students were stipended for their hours of attendance at the minimum wage rate.

As CETA expanded in the mid 1970s, the linkage established at Skills Center became the model for a county-wide job-training delivery system. Any individual who had dropped out of high school or who needed basic skills education was automatically referred to Skills Center as part of his or her employability development plan. Staff members from Skills Center and each CETA job-training program worked closely together to coordinate job and educational training activities. Enrollment at Skills Center increased to seventy students. Basic skills instruction was still at the core of the curriculum; however, other curricular areas included high school equivalency diploma preparation, English as a second language, apprenticeship and other employment-related test preparation, and tutorial support for participants who were enrolled in postsecondary vocational classes.

In addition to the development of a comprehensive curriculum, the staff recognized the need for a personalized, noninstitutional educational environment. The majority of students were young adults who had met with repeated failure in traditional educational institutions and who had negative attitudes toward learning, teachers, and schools. The lives of many were tangled in a struggle to establish independence from their families, maintain a survival income, and deal with a myriad of drug, alcohol, and police-related problems. Education was not a high priority on their list of needs and wants for survival.

Skills Center's programming and philosophy addressed the needs of this group by providing an environment that furnished the time, space, and support for students to reevaluate their negative feelings toward education and their personal feelings of inadequacy within an educational setting. The staff developed a curriculum that could be individualized to meet each student's personal goals and learning style. Instruction was designed to minimize failure and frustration, and students were encouraged to become responsible, independent learners. Personal, humanistic interaction was stressed as students were encouraged to get to know the instructors and other students in a way not possible in high school. The student-staff ratio was about seven to one. Enrollment was open-entry/open exit. Hours were scheduled, yet schedules were flexible and worked around each student's job-training schedule.

Skills Center's programming proved very successful in that the staff were able to reach many students who had previously rejected the educational system. Some students learned how to read and were able to compete for and obtain jobs from which they formerly had been excluded. A yearly average of 65 percent of General Educational Development (GED) students obtained the high school equivalency diploma. A number of students became avid and enthusiastic readers and began to read novels from cover to cover for the first time. An average of 80 percent of the participants obtained nonsubsidized employment upon leaving CETA, and 15 percent of the participants continued their education through part-time classes or full-time programs at the Madison Area Technical College.

Apart from upgrading academic skills, the most impressive accomplishment of the program was in the affective changes of many of the students. When surveyed, an overwhelming majority of students stated that they felt more confident with learning new things and more comfortable being in a school and working with a teacher. Many commented that they finally overcame lifelong math and test-taking anxieties. Everyone said they felt a greater sense of the importance of education after they completed the program than they had felt before entering it.

Skills Center was not without its problems and dissappointments. A noninstitutional, informal setting was not effective with all students. Some students, who required a more formal or structured approach, were referred to programs that could better meet their needs. Other students who were hostile to any educational environment refused to come or dropped out. All in all, these students represented less than 5 percent of the program's total population.

Many students entered Skills Center resenting the fact that educational training was a part of their CETA training plan. These students were often disruptive and uncooperative. In time, however, most accepted responsibility for their own educational objectives and became motivated to pursue them. These problems required much attention and patience from the staff. Staff members frequently found that more of their time was devoted to counseling students than to instructing them. Students frequently refused to work and preferred talking to studying. Those with more serious hostilities and internal frustrations sometimes expressed their anger physically: a slammed door, a hole punched in a wall, or a table thrown across the room.

Skills Center had no major operational problem that could not be resolved. The program was an exemplary model for basic skills instruction for young adults who had exhausted all other educational options and were no longer motivated to continue their education. It received statewide recognition for its accomplishments and was used as a model for the creation of similar programs in Wisconsin. Skills Center remained active in the CETA job-training delivery system for ten years. In the summer of 1983, when CETA legislation and programming were being phased out by Congress and when continued funding from the new Job Training Partnership Act (JTPA) was uncertain, the administration of the Madison Area Technical College decided to terminate the project.

Analyzing the Implications for Practice

The following sections describe the factors that were found to be effective in the development and implementation of the Skills Center project.

Program Philosophy. From its inception, Skills Center operated with a philosophy that committed the program to providing high-quality, humanistic education to students who had dropped out or had been expelled from traditional schools. This was accomplished by avoiding the factors that contributed to the students' negative attitudes toward school and by emphasizing learning as a positive experience.

Students were held responsible for their own education. The staff treated and respected the students as adults who could make or learn to make decisions that would affect and develop their educational potential. Students also helped to choose the methods and materials to accomplish their objectives. No student was forced to learn or work.

Some of the major tenets of the program's philosophy were to:

- Furnish a flexible environment and program structure to accommodate individual needs and schedules
- Expect students to behave as adults but not impose on them unreasonable rules or codes of conduct
- Individualize instruction so that students could work at their own pace and not compete with other students

- Base instruction on a student's abilities, not on his or her deficiencies
- Explain concepts step by step and expect to repeat them until a student thoroughly understood them
- Base expectations for a student's performance on his or her abilities and potential
- Respect students as adults and not deride them for what they do not know
- Control class size so that students received ample attention
- Encourage open discussions on any topic that was of concern to the students
- Encourage the students to know and respect the staff as human beings and not as authority figures
- Provide alternatives to students who cannot cope with academic assignments on a bad day
- Diminish a student's fears of approaching a teacher by encouraging the student to ask questions and probe ideas
- Provide as much support and human concern as possible for a student's academic, vocational, and personal development.

Structure. The program and curriculum were highly structured. Each student knew what was assigned, how to correct his or her assignments, and what to work on after an assignment was completed in case an instructor was unavailable at the moment. Most students were able to come in, get their work materials, and proceed to work without assistance.

Setting. The setting was nonthreatening. The project was located outside of a school building, first in a community center and later in a house that had been renovated into office space. The furniture was comfortable yet conducive to one-on-one instruction. Students were allowed to eat snacks or smoke. Books and magazines in all interest areas and at all reading levels were available for "free reading."

Staffing. More than any other factor, the effectiveness of the program depended on the commitment and dedication of its staff. Staff members exhibited an understanding of the issues, problems, and concerns that this group of young adults continually faced in their lives. Although the staff members were hired as instructors, a good portion of their time was devoted to counseling the students in educational, vocational, and personal matters. Each staff member had an enormous amount of patience and was able to be nonjudgmental in accepting students as individuals.

Networking. Skills Center's coordinated and cooperative linkages with other CETA programs were a valuable resource. Both the student's job-training program and Skills Center itself had an investment in the student and a concern for his or her success. This helped to assure the student's attendance, progress, and interest in the program. Furthermore, the student's duration of enrollment in CETA (about one year) permitted both programs the luxury of time to work with the student, provide some concrete job skills, and turn around some negative and destructive behaviors and attitudes.

Services. Through CETA, students were paid for their hours of attendance. Although the pay was not necessarily the motivating factor for most students to attend, it was very helpful to get students to attend in the first place and to assure, in some cases, consistent attendance. Some students were also provided transportation or given a transportation allowance to get to Skills Center by their CETA training programs.

Curriculum. The curriculum was divided into two areas: academics and life/survival skills. The academic materials were adult oriented and written at a high-interest low reading level. A variety of published and teacher-made materials was available so that instructors were not locked into giving just one set of materials to all students. The project placed little emphasis on the use of audiovisual equipment in instruction, favoring human contact over machines.

The life/survival skills materials contained a collection of instructional and informational materials on topics directly related to the personal and social needs of young adults. These materials included information on budgeting and managing finances, job seeking, apartment seeking, insurance policies, tax forms, obtaining a driver's license, family planning and birth control, health-related topics, drug and alcohol abuse, consumer awareness, current events, and a variety of other topics.

Assessment. Careful consideration was given to intake interview and assessment activities because students often formulated their strongest impressions and attitudes about the project and its staff on the first day. A staff member would privately discuss with the student his or her past experiences, future aspirations, and potential educational goals and objectives. Informal assessment techniques were used at first, instead of paper and pencil tests, to measure reading and math abilities. The process typically involved a staff member orally working through some reading and math materials with the student. Formal assessment tests were administered only after new students felt more comfortable.

Instruction. Skills Center's instructional approach was based on models for individualized instruction and student-centered teaching developed in the 1960s and early 1970s. Various curriculum development projects at that time recognized that effective teaching of basic skills required individualization (Joyce and Weil, 1972). Although some of these methods have recently been criticized as ineffective for teaching basic skills in the public schools, they did prove effective for teaching young adults throughout Skills Center's ten years of instructional programming.

Each student developed with an instructor an individualized instructional plan that considered the student's own goals, needs, and learning style. The student would then work through a series of assignments designed to teach specific concepts or skills. Instructors moved from student to student reviewing assignments and explaining new materials. If students could not demonstrate that they had learned a concept or skill, additional materials in the area would be assigned. Students moved through assignments at their own pace. Most worked independently; however, students were often encouraged to work together and to help each other. Homework was given only upon request.

Scheduling. Students were scheduled to attend an average of ten hours each week (two hours per day). Those students who could not handle that much time were scheduled for fewer hours two or three days per week. Other students were scheduled for a maximum of twenty hours each week. Enrollment was on an open-entry/open-exit basis. Most students participated in the project for between six months and one year.

Evaluation. The staff gave immediate feedback to students concerning their performance on individual assignments and their progress in general. Students were also permitted to correct their own work and monitor their own progress. Instructional plans were altered if necessary.

Twice a year, students met individually with the staff to discuss their progress. The students also had a chance at this time to evaluate the program and the effectiveness of the staff.

Summary

Providing educational programs for high school dropouts and other undereducated young adults offers many challenges to continuing education practitioners. Alternative and innovative methods to standard educational programming need to be explored if basic skills programs are to attract and keep students. Programs need to provide employability development and life/survival skills training along with the academics. Instructors need to be skilled not only in content-area teaching but also in motivating and challenging students who are frequently antagonistic to an educational system that, in their minds, had previously failed them.

Skills Center is one example of a basic skills program that was designed to address the needs of less advantaged young adults. Its strategy for successful programming was relatively simple: (1) establish a comfortable and non-threatening environment; (2) keep the program small and the student-teacher ratio low; (3) provide a curriculum relevant to the needs of the students; and (4) maintain a staff that has a tremendous amount of creativity, sensitivity, and, above all, patience.

References

Center for Public Resources. *Basic Skills in the U.S. Work Force.* New York: Center for Public Resources, 1983.

Jones, W. M. "The Impact on Society of Youths Who Drop Out or Are Undereducated." *Educational Leadership,* 1977, *34,* 411–416.

Joyce, B., and Weil, M. *Models of Teaching.* Englewood Cliffs, N.J.: Prentice-Hall, 1972.

Novak, J., and Dougherty, B. *Dropout Prevention in Wisconsin — Volume I: A Review of Programs and Activities.* Madison: Wisconsin Vocational Studies Center, University of Wisconsin–Madison, 1979.

Novak, J., and Dougherty, B. *Dropout Prevention in Wisconsin — Volume II: A Comprehensive K-12 Strategy for the School and Community.* Madison: Wisconsin Vocational Studies Center, University of Wisconsin–Madison, 1980.

William J. Buckingham is an instructor in basic education at the Madison Area Technical College and a graduate student in Continuing and Vocational Education at the University of Wisconsin–Madison.

New and innovative communication technologies can add immeasurably to already existing and future programming for young adults.

Applications of New Communication Technologies

Shirley A. White

Facilitating the learning of young adults is creating different scenarios as we respond to their learning needs by providing access to knowledge through communication technologies in individualized learning environments. This chapter examines these technologies as tools to enhance the traditional delivery of informal education. Two successful programs, conducted through Cooperative Extension in land-grant universities, are briefly examined. We also look at the potential for incorporating new technologies in order to extend these programs' usefulness to a much broader young-adult audience.

Reaching this young-adult audience, even with traditional methods, is often difficult. The complexities center around the developmental tasks of the audience itself:

- The struggle for independence, emotional maturity, and personal identity
- Decisions about career alternatives
- The selection of a mate and the need to integrate life styles and assume new roles
- The acquisition of resources for living and learning to manage them independently and effectively.

The context of reaching this age group is one where human systems are in transition and the people in them are transitory. Alienation from them-

G. G. Darkenwald, A. B. Knox (Eds.). *Meeting Educational Needs of Young Adults.* New Directions for Continuing Education, no. 21. San Francisco: Jossey-Bass, March 1984.

selves, family, the work environment, and the community is not uncommon among young adults. This generation is the television generation, and television has exposed these young adults to a wide range of life alternatives and human behaviors. There has been no dearth of television role models. However, the attempt to match models with one's own achievement often results in disappointment or despair. Winn (1977) places on the television medium the responsibility for the decline of verbal skills, the increase in escapism, and the alienation that characterize today's young adults. Changes in behavior in this generation, she says, are in the direction of noncognitive, nonactive, nonverbal thinking. Imagery, sensing (via music, for example), nonlinear and disconnected thoughts, the absence of competitive urges, and self-centered exploratory activity have emerged as new behavioral modes — the feeling dimensions.

Rather than view these changes as completely negative, the continuing educator might well accept them as clues to making changes in his or her own facilitative role and in the design of learning materials and contexts. Using new communication technologies that exploit the visual impact of TV or video and the aptness of computers for textual data can improve existing educational approaches; such use is no longer an option but a mandate.

We are living in an informative age. This implies that information is abundant, diverse, and ever present, and indeed it is. For example, satellite-delivered cable televison services now include college-credit programs, health networks, religious programming, "adult" movies, programs for investors, and much more. Paperback books abound and are available in a multitude of places — vending machines, grocery stores, airports, drugstores. Print-media distributors have a highly developed direct-mail network that reaches everyone with a mailbox. Video text, home video players (disk or tape), home computers, and new telephone services are all a part of the information revolution. At the same time, the potential for producing one's own information is constantly increasing through the use of home video cameras, do-it-yourself computer programming, and instant movies. The dilemma for the continuing educator is deciding how to use these communication technologies in order to meet important information needs as well as foster desirable changes.

Clearly, living in this information age means living with increasing complexity. The constant exposure of the young-adult generation to an explosion of knowledge, the expanding awareness resulting from thousands of hours of television viewing, and the fast track of the ever-expanding computer invasion characterize the present milieu for learning. The puzzler again, is how to capitalize on these realities in the design of educative events for young adults — and, specifically how to design events that will help them handle their developmental tasks.

Issues for Educators

It is clear that understanding the uses of the new technology requires understanding the nature of learning in relation to human growth and development. In addition, using the new technology implies changes in the educator's own behavior. In a recent paper (White, 1982), the author posed some considerations for educators, raising questions about their readiness to use new communication technologies. These considerations pointed up the importance of seeing this technology as worth exploring. Judgments have to be made as to whether the technology is appropriate for specific content and whether educators are willing to acquire the necessary resources and devote the necessary time to learning how to use it. But the key questions are: Are you willing to rethink your role as an educator and be freed from traditional, mechanical ways of handling the same material? Are you ready to change your role to a designer of learning resources, a facilitator of information, an interest stimulator, a motivator, a diagnostician of learning needs, or a dialogue initiator? The continuing educator whose methods center more clearly on the learner should find these questions and their implied role changes far less threatening than colleagues who rely on traditional delivery methods.

According to Bradford (1958, p. 141), "learning and change take place most effectively only when certain conditions are present, making it possible for the learner to enter into a process of diagnosis, experimentation, information finding, generalization, practice, and application leading toward learning, growth, and change." The personal change process parallels the learning process. Early stages are characterized by an awareness that something needs to be different. This leads to a cycle of frustration and anxiety, arguing with oneself about the relative merits of the perceived need. A period of self-exploration, risking, and testing the waters follows, often culminating in a feeling of content or relief at having faced the issue. Change, then, evolves out of such actions as testing out new behaviors, acquiring new information, and applying it to perceived problems. Insights begin to develop, and the new behavior or new learning begins to be integrated into thought and action. The final stage of this change process results in establishing generalizations or principles for handling experiences in the future.

Internal conflict characterizes the change process and learning is painful at times. If the acquisition of information requires adjustment to new learning technology as well as to new content, then behavior changes will require even more time and patience — giving up old, comfortable ways of believing, thinking, and valuing is not easy. However, mastery (of both the technology and the content) leads to heightened pleasure in discovery and tends to motivate further change.

Benefits of New Technologies

Incorporation of video and computer technologies represents a change in many dimensions for the educator and the learner. Both are adjusting to new tools, shedding old modes of knowledge acquisition. For the learner, video is capable of handling a diversity of tasks. For the educator, it can be a basic audiovisual support or play a more active role in the learning process.

Simple video feedback can be used to monitor teaching effectiveness, to aid in one-to-one counseling, to assist in recall, to document, or to carry messages. Some of the most powerful uses of video involve conflict intervention and psychiatric counseling. There is no substitute for the power of real images.

Video is in itself integrative, capable of incorporating all forms of audio or visual formats—for example, still photographs, film, music, slides, graphics, and narration. Coupled with the power of computers, video expands both learners' and educators' capacity for data retrieval. With imaginative designers, these technologies can serve almost any conceivable educative need.

The use of these technologies does imply role changes, new configurations of episodes in the learning context, and changes in the planning of curriculum or training agendas. These changes offer increased opportunities to involve learners in problem solving and in selecting content that is tailored to their unique needs. Using the video disk, simulations, and imaginative computer programming for education must also take into account individual learning styles. Thus, the communication technologies can provide educational methods that are more learner centered than the traditional techniques.

Interestingly, the fear of these technologies as a source of educative help is close to nil in the young adult, due to exposure in early childhood and in the ensuing years prior to adult educative pursuits. Conversely, the prospect of using these tools may produce apprehension in the continuing educator and may require great personal courage and a restructuring of self-images related to the teaching role.

A Model for Young-Adult Programming

Tough (1971) defined self-directed learning as deliberate engagement in "learning episodes." Participation is intentional, involving pursuit of definite knowledge and skill to be retained or used over a definite period of time. From the research and writing of many continuing educators, self-directedness appears to be a key to young-adult educability and is an absolute necessity for selecting the learning resources available through new communication technologies. Skager (1978) synthesizes and cites additional constructs that relate to self-directedness:

- Self-acceptance—positive views about self as learner
- Planfulness—able to diagnose own needs, set goals, and select strategy
- Intrinsic motivation—rewards derive from the learning process
- Internal evaluation—accurate assessment of own performance
- Openness to experience—curiosity, tolerance for ambiguity, preference for complexity, even playfulness may be basic to motivation .
- Flexibility—willingness and ability to change
- Autonomy—can make learning episode selection independent from expectations of others.

These insights, coupled with knowledge of young-adult developmental tasks and skills, open a new perspective on approaches to young-adult programming and to the design of learning resources that integrate the new technologies.

As young persons move through the maturation process, their self-concept develops toward increasing self-sufficiency and self-directedness. Moreover, the accumulation of experience provides an ever-increasing and ever-changing base for new learning. Motivation to learn also becomes more pragmatic and problem centered (Knowles, 1980). Experiencing, experimenting, and discussing are characteristic of the process. While young adults wrestle with developmental tasks, intense pressures come from all directions — self, peers, parents, family members, employers, and significant others in the community or in the work environment. These pressures result in stress, which in turn requires some sort of adaptive behavior if it is to be resolved. Newly perceived educational needs are often the outcome of this process. It is at this point that the young adult is motivated to educative action, and the continuing educator should be in a position to respond, helping him or her to articulate more fully these needs. If in fact there is to be a meaningful dialogue, it is likely to be related directly to the extent of self-directedness in the young adult.

Capitalizing on this dialogue, learners and educators can interact to pursue a program designed in the traditional fashion — that is, by defining the focus, audience, level of content, implementation, and so on. However, the model advocated here urges the selection of delivery channels that are new; this means exploring such new alternatives as electronic technology, used alone or interfaced with traditionally mediated materials and learning environments. New alternatives require a supportive environment and a wide range of self-paced learner choices and interactive exercises, and they demand a high degree of learner control. Immediate feedback with positive reinforcement and with gentle, nonthreatening inputs is desirable. Inherent in this model, then, is the assumption that learning "episodes" should be tailored to individual need, allowing nonjudgmental responses to self-assessment. In this way, learning will be maximized and the young adult freed to create new directions and uncover his or her own learning resources in the future.

The practical implications of this model can be more fully appreciated by considering its potential for enhancing traditional programs for young adults. To that end, two successful programs are described in the following sections, both of which employ traditional rather than technologically based delivery systems. The case studies form the basis for the concluding section, which discusses how communication technology could extend the reach and effectiveness of these and similar programs and describes the changes in current practice necessary if this is to occur.

Sewing for Profit

Traditionally, Cooperative Extension Service home economics programs have helped families make efficient use of their personal and economic resources in order to improve their quality of life. Clothing construction has always been an important and popular program offering. Joyce Smith, clothing specialist at Ohio State University, has capitalized on this traditional interest and has given it an innovative twist, resulting in significant financial gains for young homemakers and increased feelings of self-worth and identity.

The program is called "Sewing for Profit." Its participants are those home sewers who have enthusiastically used their sewing skills to extend their families' clothing budget. Joyce Smith, through county home economists, has shown these sewers that home sewing can produce much-needed supplementary income or even be parlayed into a full-time small business.

Since the fall of 1979, the program has conducted workshops at some two dozen locations in Ohio with more than 3,500 persons attending. The target audience was loosely identified as those persons already engaged in, or thinking about starting, home-based sewing-related businesses. Homemakers with young children were targeted, especially those whose children would require daycare services if both parents worked outside the home. Smith attributes the success of the program to the fact that she and her colleagues accurately assessed the need among homemakers with whom they had contact and who had participated in other clothing-related programs.

There were three innovative aspects of this continuing education program: First, the program addressed the business aspects and family concerns of custom sewing businesses rather than simply individual skill development. Second, the design phase of the program not only included the target homemakers and the county home economists (a usual combination) but also received input from the College of Administrative Science at Ohio State University, the U.S. Small Business Administration, and the Social Security Administration. Third, local workshops involved people from the area's Small Business Administration and individuals who had successfully engaged in custom sewing. Smith gave presentations entitled "Is Custom Sewing for You?" and "Selling Strategies." Participants were left with very specific advice on establishing their businesses and on where to go for help. They were also given the opportunity to request more comprehensive information related to specific business goals.

County home economists have provided follow-up programs. Ellen Teller in Darke County is typical. Specific topics handled in that county during the first year of follow up were quilting, sewing and fitting, upholstery, and sewing children's clothing. But the major event was the organization of a craft cooperative to help homemakers market their handiwork; the cooperative was designed both for those who operated at a business level and those who wanted supplemental income. The group anticipates lots of work and at least three years to get its cooperative off the ground, but the pilot events gave the sewers a much better idea of how to market crafts and of the business aspects of home marketing. This continuing education program not only has motivated job-related learning but also has resulted in business organizations that will have an impact on the broader community.

Smith believes that virtually every skill related to home economics can be marketed. Such ventures as catering services, daycare of the elderly, tag-sale planning, and small home-appliance repair are typical. The home business concept is consistent with predictions for the information age, centering more labor-intensive activity in the home, using data available from personal computers, cable television, and home versions of the automated office. Computer terminals might well allow the homebound young adult to perform accounting or secretarial services, taking dictation via telephone, transcribing at home, and entering data into information-processing terminals. A little later in this chapter, we look at other ways in which the new technologies could expand the impact and effectiveness of a program like Sewing for Profit.

On Your Own

A program developed by Dian Naphis for Onondaga County Cooperative Extension in New York State addresses the financial insecurities of young adults. New York State is plagued by unemployment, and young men and women are the hardest hit due to the prevailing "last-hired, first-hired" philosophy and the difficulty of obtaining a job in the first place. According to Jeanne Hogarth, a consumer economist in the College of Human Ecology, Cornell University, the problems of unemployment and inflation are not going to go away soon. "And the young audience isn't going away either. Demographics indicate we're going to see large numbers in the nineteen to twenty-five age group," Hogarth says. She acts as a resource and support for Cooperative Extension Service agents in New York State and cites Naphis's program as one effort to counteract the serious negative consequences of unemployment and inflation.

The program is a letter series on topics vital to young people trying to establish financial independence for the first time. Titled "On Your Own," the series features well-written, practical advice on such topics as choosing and furnishing an apartment, sharing housing with friends and pets, saving on energy costs, refining budget skills to make the most of cash flow, and getting "more for your money" when shopping. Such concerns as what to do when you lose your job, protecting your credit, starting a bank account, and borrowing money are also covered. The letters are short, four-page publications, in two-column format, with attractive illustrations and readable type.

Piloted in Onondaga County under the leadership of Carol Wixson, the series is distributed to subscribers who request it at nominal cost. Because of time and personnel constraints, no extraordinary efforts have been made to market the series. A one-page flyer and order blank are available in supermarkets, social service agencies, and other public places. The series is also on display in the Cooperative Extension Office in Syracuse, which sees a large number of consumers coming in to gather all kinds of information. Response has been generally favorable, with over 100 subscribers to date. Wixson plans to do an evaluative follow-up over time, assessing the long-term effects of the letters' advice on young people who have used them.

Implications of Technology for Program Delivery and for Practitioners

Programs such as the two described, which meet basic young-adult developmental needs and which have a concrete body of content, are those that can be readily adapted for delivery via "packaged" media. Much of the content can be delivered through real images, suggesting that video can be used effectively. The ideas of a content expert, for example, can reach more people through his or her presence on videotape or disk. Those 3,500 home business entrepreneurs in Ohio may be ready for more in-depth information that can be delivered on video and then used in self-determined fashion individually or in their networking groups.

Information on consumer concerns (like that provided through the mail by On Your Own) also lends itself well to video; interactive video could reinforce principles of money and other resource management. The provider, in this case county extension organizations, should alter delivery systems to include such media in the future.

In order to make the changes necessary for incorporating new communication technologies, continuing educators must acquire new knowledge and skills, restructure their roles, and accept the notion of becoming what Lippitt (1982) terms a "renewal facilitator." The first order of business is to bring about changes in organizational systems so new modes of operation can replace old ones. As a learning specialist, the facilitator must have the ability to apply learning theory to up-to-date communication media that will meet the fast-changing needs of specific clientele. For professionals to stay up to date and competent, Lippitt urges them to develop a strategy for their own continued growth. Strategies include seeking feedback data to incorporate into every aspect of the work role. Utilizing team or codeveloper relationships can produce the stimulation and reinforcement often needed for this kind of change. Documenting activities, making presentations, and publishing tend to be stimulants. Formal learning episodes, affiliation with professional organizations, informal collegial networking, internships, and sabbaticals also are useful strategies. Perhaps the most critical notion about changing or upgrading competencies is the conscious development and writing down of a self-development plan, complete with target dates, ideas for resource acquisition, and reading programs — all in detail.

Changing either organizational or individual human "systems" requires acquisition of new skills and new ways to manage stress and conflict, both external and internal. Setting aside the time and making the commitment to do it is the challenge. If young adults are to reap the greatest possible benefits of enlightened assistance from educators such as those in Cooperative Extension, it is quite clear that systems renewal must take place — and quickly. Successful programs such as the two described here are in place all over the United States. Constrained by lack of money, time, or personnel resources, the programs may not reach their potential for maximum impact, but by capitalizing on visual and computer power, these programs for young adults can become increasingly learner centered and cost effective.

References

Bradford, L. P. "The Teaching-Learning Transaction." *Adult Education,* 1958, *8* (3), 135–145.

Knowles, M. S. *The Modern Practice of Adult Education.* (Rev. ed.). Chicago: Follett, 1980.

Lippitt, G. *Organizational Renewal.* Englewood Cliffs, N.J.: Prentice-Hall, 1982.

Skager, R. *Lifelong Education and Evaluation Practice.* Elmsford, N.Y.: Pergamon Press, 1978.

Tough, A. *The Adult's Learning Projects.* Toronto: Ontario Institute for Studies in Education, 1971.

White, S. A. "Interactive Video: Concepts and Considerations." Paper presented at the New Technology Show, Cornell University, Nov. 1982.

Winn, M. *The Plug-In Drug.* New York: Bantam, 1977.

Shirley A. White is professor of communication arts, College of Agriculture and Life Sciences, Cornell University. She has also served as the state leader, Home Economics Extension, Kansas State University, and as an associate director of New York State Cooperative Extension, Cornell University.

The preceding chapters raise issues that require both deliberation and action.

Themes and Issues in Programming for Young Adults

Gordon G. Darkenwald
Alan B. Knox

Despite the diversity of topics addressed in the various chapters of this volume, several recurring themes and issues are discernible. These themes and issues comprise the substance of this concluding chapter, which attempts to spell out their implications for deliberation and debate as well as for professional practice. The first matter discussed concerns the apparent neglect—both in the literature and in practice—of young adults as a distinctive population for continuing education programming.

Young Adults: A Neglected Species?

Few continuing educators would deny that adults at different stages of the life span differ in development characteristics that are important for planning and implementing responsive programs. Why, then, is so much attention, both in the literature and in developmentally targeted programming, lavished on the middle-aged and elderly and apparently so little on the young? Particularly striking is that education for older adults has become an established specialization with its own journal (*Educational Gerontology*) and its own interest groups within continuing education and related professional associations. This phenomenon can, of course, be explained and justified, but it is

G. G. Darkenwald, A. B. Knox (Eds.). *Meeting Educational Needs of Young Adults.* New Directions for Continuing Education, no. 21. San Francisco: Jossey-Bass, March 1984.

noted here to underscore what seems to be the second class citizenship of adults at the opposite pole of the life-span continuum. The basic issue, therefore, is: What are the reasons for the apparent neglect of young adults?

A close reading of this volume suggests at least a partial answer. The heart of the matter is that young adulthood as defined here (that is, from age sixteen or seventeen to approximately age thirty-four) is not a unitary phenomenon. Virtually every chapter in this sourcebook either states or implies that persons in their late teens and early twenties are rarely adults in the full sense of the word. They have been referred to as "Stage 1 adults" or "younger young adults," but these circumlocutions simply obscure the reality that "late adolescent" is a more accurate label for the majority of this group. It might also be said that if late adolescents are not "adult enough," persons in their mid twenties to mid thirties are "too adult" in the sense that they are prototypical, constituting the prime age category for most providers of continuing education. Moreover, since they suffer neither the handicaps of old age nor the often wrenching adjustments of mid life, their distinctive needs are easily obscured by the misguided perception that they are simply "normal adults," a category decidedly devoid of meaning.

Are, then, young adults a neglected species? The answer, it seems, is largely yes — but with some important qualifications. Clearly, school dropouts and noncollege-bound high school graduates are, in many ways, neglected for reasons that are understandable if not justifiable. This conclusion and its implications will be discussed later in this chapter in more detail. Mature young adults in their twenties and early thirties quite evidently are not neglected, if one applies such criteria as the availability of appropriate educational opportunities and high rates of participation. However, one might question the extent to which current programs address the full range of developmental issues and tasks of this age group, particularly in respect to its least-advantaged members.

In brief, then, young adults are to some degree a neglected species, primarily because an age-range definition cannot be reconciled with developmental differences within that range — differences that are reflected in such concepts as identity, independence, and maturity.

The Significance of Developmental Characteristics

A pervasive theme discussed or illustrated in every chapter is the importance for effective practice of understanding and applying knowledge related to young-adult development. The challenges and transitions of this stage of the life span lie at the heart of planning responsive programs. Of course, this observation is a commonplace in the literature and is applicable to all adults, not just the young. However, there is reason to question the extent to which it is actually translated into practice or even seriously considered in the planning of continuing education activities. Many of the problems addressed by the contributors to this volume would not exist, or would be less serious, if continuing educators dutifully heeded this fundamental admonition. Compelling evidence for this conclusion can be found in the chapters by Smith and Buckingham, as well as in others.

A more subtle but still related issue is how the term "adult development" is understood. The general interpretation seems to be that it refers to the developmental tasks common to persons at a particular stage of the life cycle (such tasks as choosing a career or coping with retirement) or to the performance demands of generic adult roles involving marriage, work, parenthood, and so forth. But as Merriam points out in the first chapter, adult development is not limited to these sociocultural tasks; it also includes psychological issues such as independence, identity, and intimacy. Moreover, for late adolescents, or very young adults, these and other psychological factors are particularly salient because their resolution is a necessary condition for negotiating the transition to full adult status (Bocknek, 1980).

The need for continuing educators to be sensitive to these psychological issues is illustrated by Smith's case study of GED students in Chapter Four. However, organized efforts to help young adults negotiate these critical psychological passages are rare indeed. Developing programs to meet needs of this nature can be difficult, but precedents exist in programs targeted for the middle-aged and elderly. For example, continuing education activities for very young men and women can help them prepare for adulthood by addressing both internal concerns (independence, identity, intimacy) and external roles (occupation, family, interpersonal relations). For Stage 1 young adults, methods that include interaction with peers and younger people (such as a youth-group leader) may be more effective than interaction mainly with middle-aged adults. By contrast, Stage 2 young adults with children of their own may have a new appreciation and interest in relations with middle-aged adults.

Education for Adult Roles

Continuing education programs can be more responsive and have greater impact by relating directly to adult role performance. Education for improved role performance is especially important but problematical for some young adults. For example, for young people who are employed or optimistic about their chances for employment, occupation-related continuing education is widespread and is the main reason for educational participation. But what could be done to attract and serve Stage 1 young adults who are not employed? Family-life education is of interest to many young adults, but what could be done for those who are single? Participation rates in continuing education for community problem solving are lower for very young adults than for adults beyond age twenty-five or thirty who have gained a sense of the importance of community issues and services for themselves, their children, family, and friends. What can be done to help young adults use continuing education as they start to recognize their stake in community problem solving? Responsive programs appeal to the multiple motives (noted in the second chapter by Darkenwald) that increase the likelihood of participation. Decision to participate and progress (or not) reflect multiple influences, some internal (personal) and some external (situational). For example, Smith's chapter described young GED students who admired but did not emulate older more persistent and hard-working students. The young GED students appear similar to the television generation characterized in White's chapter as escapist, prone to nonverbal and disconnected thinking, uncompetitive, and self-centered. By contrast, the older GED students seem more like the successful young managers described in Greenstein's chapter as eager to learn and willing to admit mistakes, accept help, and work hard. How can we help Stage 1 young adults to use continuing education to accelerate the transition to Stage 2?

Comprehensive Approach

Continuing education practitioners who want to serve hard-to-reach young adults, such as those with little formal education, self-confidence, group affiliation, or employment prospects face formidable problems. Successful approaches to serving hard-to-reach adults tend to be comprehensive, responsive to their life-styles, and take mutltiple internal and external influences into account (Darkenwald and Larson, 1980). The following paragraphs describe components of such a comprehensive approach.

Persuasive Communication. Procedures to encourage participation should use various channels with an emphasis on oral communication from people that nonparticipants know and trust. Human-interest stories about young adults who are similar to the nonparticipants and who have found continuing education useful can be especially influential. Personal contact is especially effective because adults with little formal education are unlikely to know participants or to use mass media to seek information related to continuing education opportunities.

Reduction of Barriers. Chapter Two by Darkenwald listed barriers to occupationally related continuing education (such as inertia, costs, insufficient benefits, and family or work constraints). Practitioners who want to serve hard-to-reach adults should try to reduce such barriers as well as help young adults themselves to do so.

Relevant Content. Perhaps the most important component of a comprehensive approach are program topics that young adults perceive as relevant to their developmental tasks. Examples include goal-related subject matter content that applies directly to decisions regarding obtaining and advancing in desirable jobs or to family life and childcare.

Responsive Methods. Even though some young adults disliked school, the desire for familiarity and security contributes in many cases to expressed preferences for traditional methods of learning. Practitioners can gradually introduce informal, interactive, individualized, and supportive methods of teaching and learning that are responsive to their preferred learning styles and that help them learn how to learn and how to use more varied methods. Buckingham's chapter listed implications for practice from the Skills Center that indicate specific characteristics of responsive methods.

Formative Evaluation. Practitioners who want to serve hard-to-reach young adults whom they have not attracted before can combine needs assessment information with formative evaluation. Findings from such evaluations can contribute to gradual program improvement.

Multiple Providers. Sometimes a provider can most effectively reach hard-to-reach adults by cooperating with other organizations. Such cooperation includes cosponsorship with other providers and referrals from community agencies. An especially productive partnership links institutions that have educational resources with organizations that have young adult members, employees, or clients.

The Ultimate Challenge

At this juncture, the most troubling issue should be clear—namely, that there are two species subsumed by the category of "young adult." One ranges in age from the mid twenties to the early thirties. To be sure, it has certain distinctive characteristics and needs, but it poses no extraordinary challenge to the creativity and skills of most continuing educators. The other species is less familiar to the majority of practitioners and likely to remain so. But for those to whom it is familiar, it can pose a host of problems. This species, of course, is the late adolescent, or the "not-quite-adult," and its characteristics are also distinct.

Now that the two species have been identified, the metaphor can be discarded and some troublesome questions considered. However, it should first be noted that not all young people in their teens and early twenties are dependent adolescents. This is especially true of many noncollege-bound high school graduates like those described by Knox in Chapter Three. Of concern here are recent school dropouts enrolled in basic skills, GED, and job-training programs. Very few can be considered adults if only because their handicaps prevent them from establishing psychological and financial independence.

In regard to this group of young persons, several fundamental issues need to raised even though they cannot be fully explicated in this chapter. First, should continuing educators accept responsibility for serving an adolescent clientele? This, of course, is primarily a value question. It merits deliberation because continuing education, at least in theory, is concerned with facilitating *adult* learning and has generally eschewed the task of socializing preadults, which is presumably the business of schools and colleges. Second, *can* continuing educators avoid this responsibility even if, in principle, it *should* be avoided?

This, of course, is principally a practical and political question. Given the mandates of the Adult Education Act and other legislation that defines adults broadly to include late adolescents, the answer seems to be "no." Needless to say, continuing educators can choose to give priority to recruiting and serving mature adults, in effect consigning late adolescents to a condition of "benign neglect." Whether this alternative is feasible (in relation to enrollments) or ethical is open to debate. Finally, if responsibility for serving late adolescents should not or cannot be avoided, then the relevant issue is, how can continuing educators best meet the needs of this clientele? The chapters in this sourcebook suggest many insights and practical guidelines pertinent to this question. The following suggestions are merely illustrative:

1. Be sensitive to the fact that late adolescents are going through a period of internal turmoil as they negotiate the difficult passage to full adult status. "Immature" attitudes and behavior are symptomatic manifestations of the struggle for identity and independence.

2. Provide a warm and flexible learning environment. The continuing education program should bear as little resemblance to the structure and social climate of the typical high school as possible.

3. Do not expect instant, positive adjustment to a more learner-centered environment. Dysfunctional attitudes and behaviors acquired in school take time to unlearn.

4. Make clear what you expect from the students and what they can expect from program staff. Communicate forcefully that students are responsible for their own learning, for adhering to reasonable standards of conduct, and for taking initiative in discussing their problems with teachers or counselors.

5. To the extent possible, provide an individualized instructional program for each student—the more individual attention the better. Continuous, constructive feedback on performance is essential. Flexibility and individual responsibility should not, however, be confused with lack of structure. The latter is essential in working with this population, despite the fact that such structure is often resisted.

6. Provide a curriculum relevant to the distinctive needs of this population. The "three R's" are seldom sufficient. Attention should be given to career development in the broad sense of the term as well as to survival or coping skills. Emphasis on the latter is associated with higher atttendance and lower dropout rates in adult basic skills programs (Darkenwald, 1975).

7. In addition to ongoing informal counseling on an individual basis, consider providing group counseling for both emotional support purposes and as a means of identifying and resolving existing or potential problems.

8. Finally, avoid age-segregated instruction unless the late-adolescent group is so disruptive that it interferes with classroom learning and alienates older, more serious students. If this is not the case, age segregation is undesirable because it deprives adolescents of adult role models and can result in their feeling stigmatized, thus reinforcing alienation and further undermining self-esteem, motivation, and striving for independence. (The benefits of association with a broader age range of adults depend on keeping the late adolescents to a minority of participants so that the climate and pacing are set by the older students.)

Summary

For reasons discussed at the beginning of this chapter, the education of young adults is not an established field of specialization nor is it likely to attain this status. Consequently, practitioners interested in developing effective programs for this clientele face considerable difficulties in locating resources for helping them do so. There is no substantial body of professional literature to turn to, no special interest groups of like-minded continuing educators to offer assistance and support. Despite these obstacles, the situation is not desperate. The references following each chapter in this volume provide one important resource for acquiring further information. In addition, the ERIC system contains numerous documents related to specific issues, sponsoring agencies, and young-adult populations. Finally, there is nothing to prevent continuing educators in any sector of the field from organizing formal or informal interest groups under the auspices of professional associations committed to the principle of lifelong learning.

References

Bocknek, G. *The Young Adult.* Monterey, Calif.: Brooks/Cole, 1980.
Darkenwald, G. "Some Effects of the 'Obvious Variable': Teachers' Race and Holding Power with Black Adult Students." *Sociology of Education,* 1975, *48,* 420–431.
Darkenwald, G., and Larson, G. *Reaching Hard-to-Reach Adults.* New Directions for Continuing Education, no. 8. San Francisco: Jossey-Bass, 1980.

Gordon G. Darkenwald is professor of adult and continuing education at Rutgers University.

Alan B. Knox is professor of continuing education at the University of Wisconsin–Madison.

Index